D1596916

FORSITAN MEMINESSE UIVABIT.

REMINISCENCES

BY

DR. W. G. CURTIS,

1848-1900.

FOR THIRTY YEARS STATE QUARANTINE

SURGEON FOR THE PORT OF WILMINGTON.

HERALD JOB OFFICE.

SOUTHPORT, N. C.

Printed In the United States of America
ISBN 1-892444-11-9
Second Edition
March 1999

The title page approximates the layout in the original 1905 printing

Published by
Southport Historical Society, Inc.
501 North Atlantic Avenue
Southport, North Carolina 28461-3503

FOREWORD

In June of 1997 my father, Nathaniel Cortlandt Curtis, passed away. He was the son and namesake of the middle son of Walter Gilman Curtis and his wife Margaret, both longtime residents of Southport. "Buster," as my father was affectionately known to family and friends, had inherited a most unique desk upon the passing of his father in 1952, and we know that this desk belonged to Margaret Coit Curtis, and probably to her mother. Being the eldest of seven children, I was deemed the appropriate beneficiary of the desk, and it now sits in the living room of my home in Flat Rock, North Carolina.

The desk held no interest for our generation until about ten years ago. My father began familiarizing us with our heritage, through a family newsletter, by publishing stories and information in installments, thereby piquing our curiosity. All of these accounts came from records and manuscripts which had been stored in the desk for many years. Some of my siblings and I took the bait and have been inexorably fascinated with tracing our roots ever since.

Two particularly significant writings that have influenced my genealogical journey are a set of three diaries that were kept by Margaret Curtis during the years 1886 through 1896, detailing everyday life in Southport, and a thin, brown soft-cover book entitled *Reminiscences of Wilmington and Smithville---Southport*, written by Dr. Walter Curtis and published by his son Howard in Southport in 1905. These recountings have led our family to make several trips to Southport where we attempted to envision and experience the lives of our ancestors.

Several pleasant outcomes were derived from our journeys to

Southport. On our first visit there, we found that the town had changed little since just before the turn of the century, and had still retained its charm and allure as described in Margaret's diaries and Walter's reminiscences. Although some of the landmarks we had read about no longer existed, it was easy to visualize where they once stood and how they looked. A lot of this experience was made possible by the efforts of the Southport Historical Society to preserve the history and beauty of this quaint town.

On a subsequent trip to Southport, we were received with such hospitality by Susan Carson, long time historian of the town, and by Wolf and Mary Furstenau, relative newcomers to the area, but no less enthusiastic about the accounts of Southport and surrounding areas. These people have become our friends and provide us with another link to Southport.

In 1909, my great uncle, Howard C. Curtis, wrote in an editorial for the *Southport Herald*: "When any well informed observer notices a disposition on the part of municipal authorities to preserve and safeguard natural decorative features such as trees and to perpetuate historical landmarks unaltered and to add various improvements that will tend to make a town more attractive, he realizes that that town is destined always to have a unique individuality and charm above other towns." Southport has retained that unique individuality and charm, a heritage of which the people of this town can be proud.

Carol Curtis Kemper
February 1999

INTRODUCTION

This reprint of *Reminiscences of Wilmington and Smithville-Southport, 1848-1900* by Dr. Walter Gilman Curtis was undertaken as part of a wide-ranging effort by members of the Southport Historical Society, Inc. to make available to researchers—and those interested in local history—literature through which the pages of history assume meaning and perspective.

Changes to the text of the original edition were made sparingly. Obvious typographical errors were corrected, as well as occasional errors made by the author, which appear correct elsewhere in the text. Capitalization of words and spellings that differ from contemporary usage were left intact to preserve the tenor of the time. For example, the Civil War in the 1860s was a civil war to Curtis and his contemporaries. An index, not present in the original, was added as an aid to researchers and those interested in genealogy.

Curtis elaborates on a number of ideas that were extremely topical and much discussed at the time. One is the emergence of Wilmington as the seaport to which Smithville aspired but failed to bring to fruition. He wistfully belabors the passing of the 'good old days,' i.e., the half-century ante-bellum era, exemplified by the landed gentility and the laid-back lifestyle of small-town Smithville which proved so inviting to Wilmington visitors. The misguided ambitions of Brunswick County farmers to forsake all for the production of turpentine receives admonition and lament. Finally, Curtis becomes irascible in his description of the machinations of the Republicans during Reconstruction. But at the age of 79, when the *Reminiscences* were published, the man who spent a lifetime in public service sees hope in the new generation, the change from sail to coal-fired cargo vessels, and the emergence of cotton as the new gift of the land.

WF

Figure 1. Dr. Walter Gilman Curtis.

Photo courtesy Southport Pythagoras Masonic Lodge

CHAPTER ONE

In the year of 1848 and from that time on until 1861, Wilmington was in her zenith of prosperity as the greatest naval-store producer in the world. A traveler coming down the line of the Wilmington & Weldon Railroad, and having almost arrived, and could congratulate himself on having escaped the dangers of a journey upon those rails which existed, not only on that railroad but nearly every other railroad in the country, with a mind free from anxiety would be likely to ask "what was the mean[ing] of that dense cloud which hung over the city as if escaping from the horrible Stygian smoke from the pit which is bottomless?" and he would be told, that that was the smoke caused by the manufacture of turpentine into various articles which are commercially designated by the name of naval stores in which is included tar, pitch, rosin, and spirits turpentine; and being interested in what was new to him he would say he must go immediately and investigate the business. Having arrived at his hotel in the city, and as is customary, having been introduced to all the bystanders, and established a record as a friend to all mankind especially the southern mankind, he would take a bath to rid himself of smoke, and cinders which accompanied at that time the traveler on railroads, he would take a good supper and come down into the waiting room of the hotel, to continue the friendship so pleasantly initiated on his arrival. The next morning he would take a trip around the city, and would find its business to consist mostly of saw mills, turpentine distilleries to carry away the product of which the wharves were lined with vessels, mostly schooners in the coastwise trade, and on the street bordering the river on the wharves, commission merchants dealing in lumber, and naval stores. These he would find to be men of large experience in that line of business. He would be told that the raw turpentine used in the manufacture of these articles before mentioned was extracted from the pine trees with which the country was covered for many miles, and which lined every creek, river and estuary in the eastern part of North Carolina. Being inclined to examine further into this business he would employ the services of a carriage, and driver, or perhaps a saddle horse, and would go across the ferry to the mainland beyond, from whence he would continue his journey toward Shallotte. At every turn he would meet negroes with the tools necessary to cut into the trees that the turpentine might run out therefrom, and he would be surprised to hear the musical yodling which resounded through the woods in every direction that it seemed to him for miles away, and he would conclude, that the makers of turpentine were a set of men who made themselves happy by this peculiar yodling as they passed from tree to tree hacking each till each negro had finished his task, which was to hack ten thousand boxes or trees, once a week. You would see the turpentine running down the tree into boxes notched for catching it, then where the trees are hacked more than one year, he would see the white face of the tree as far as his eye could reach, stopping at night with a turpentine farmer who was always glad to see him, and invite him to partake of his hospitality. As the negroes came in from their work at night, they continued their yodling until the woods resounded, and when some happy, and melodious sound could be heard everywhere. The whole country seemed to be devoted to this business; there were few fields of corn to be seen or any other crop, for the turpentine farmer was engrossed in the occupation of making turpentine. Near every dwelling house, there was to be seen a cooper's shed, where the rough barrels were made for containing turpentine; when the barrels were filled with this product of the forest, the mules, and the wagons would be brought out, and the barrels would be hauled to the nearest landing place, and from thence transported to Wilmington where the owner would probably be waiting to receive his money, turpentine always being sold for cash on delivery. The peculiarities of this business which a traveler would observe, were that the negroes were always fat, slick, and greasy and consequently happy; that the farmer himself had plenty of money and generally had a large roll of bills in his pocket, and expected the business to be always prosperous. The business of making turpentine was an immense one in the city of Wilmington, and the harbor was usually crowded with vessels of all sizes, and descriptions except large vessels, of which there were few or none; they generally carried from two thousand to four thousand barrels, and the river being full of shoals these were obliged to have skillful pilots to get them to sea. This was Wilmington in her palmy days of the naval-store trade. As may be readily imagined this business could not last forever as when the trees were once drained of their sap they were worthless for most purposes, and so with the end of the naval store business the lumber business could also see its end approaching because these trees did not make valuable lumber when sawed. So in the year 1861 the whole business was at an end during the years of war, and reconstruction. After civil government was re-established both the naval store, and lumber business recommenced with great vigor, but its time of prosperity was nearly at an end for want of the material which had been used for this trade and Wilmington saw its business decline, so that where once the docks were lined with vessels there were but few. In this crisis of commercial affairs Wilmington had to look around for a substitute, but there was none apparent. Fortunately there were a few merchants of great business experience who started the cotton trade, of which before this time there had been none, and so successful did they make it, that at the present time there is nearly four hundred thousand bales exported from Wilmington yearly. But naval stores did not build up a city, although it was a prosperous business. Neither did the lumber business build up the city to any extent, and it is also true, that the mere exportation of cotton will not build up a city. Its growth was slow up to 1861, but after the war was over it has seemed to prosper in the building of public buildings and private residences, in the improvement of its streets and thoroughfares, in its water supply and in its electric lighting, a long step was made along the line of improvement. During all this time which I have described the social conditions prevailing in Wilmington, and Smithville were very attractive in their nature. The gentlemen of Wilmington were friendly, and hospitality entertained in every household. The ladies were gentle, refined, and beautiful, and once they had taken a stranger to be their friend the kindly relations lasted through life. Alas! all or nearly all, of

3

the class I have described of that generation have gone to their last resting place, but their memories are fresh and green, and to be handed down to succeeding generations. With this passing tribute to friends of the long ago I pass on to another chapter of events disconnected with any kind of business but which were full of interest in their time but which more especially refers to the Smithville of those days.

CHAPTER TWO

Smithville was reached from Wilmington by the line of ocean steamers which were a continuation of the great line to the south. These were four steamers named "The Gladiator," the "C. Vanderbilt," the "Governor Dudley," the "North Carolina," the last of which was a spare ship to be used in case of accident to any of the others. They were commanded respectively by Captain Isaac B. Smith, Captain Sterrit, and Capt. Bates, and were very popular, making their trips for many years to Charleston, South Carolina without accident. They started daily from Wilmington on the arrival of the northern train. Breakfast, and dinner were served on board between Wilmington, and Smithville, and they were fine repasts as they had the markets of Charleston, and Wilmington to rely upon, with all the luxuries they afforded. These steamships took passengers, and freight for Smithville, and made their landing at a wharf near where the steamer Wilmington now has her landing. Returning from Charleston they stopped at the same wharf and breakfast served between Smithville, and Wilmington. I will here mention the name of a woman quite celebrated in the annals of Smithville; her name was Mrs. Mary Duffy, who kept an eating house on the water's edge, which was long patronized by the citizens of Smithville, especially by the pilots. For over twenty five years Mrs. Duffy arose about three o'clock in the morning, and prepared breakfast for all passengers intending to go up in the steamer. A cup of coffee, or anything else wanted by the pilots, who wanted a morning meal before going to sea in search for vessels. There were several fine deck boats which were very fast, and able to go to sea in all weather; each of these pilot boats carried as many pilots as were necessary, and sometimes did not come into port again until they had put all their pilots aboard of incoming vessels. The bar at that time had about 12 feet of water upon it, consequently vessels coming into this port must be of that draft, and built to carry from 1900 to 2000 barrels of naval stores; they also brought from the northern markets what ever freight was offered, and this was nearly all the northern freight because the railroad was very uncertain. Mrs. Duffy was remarkable in her powers of seeing and hearing, and her business was, in addition to supplying meals to wake up passengers who wished to take the steamer to Wilmington as these steamers entered port before light in the morning. It was necessary that Mrs. Duffy go by the sense of hearing, and she could always hear these boats which were side wheelers, far enough out to sea to enable the passengers she had collected to get up and dress, and go down to her establishment for a cup of coffee before going on the steamship wharf; as may be well imagined Mrs. Duffy was a very important character in the life of Smithville, and she was duly appreciated by all the citizens of Smithville as a good, and faithful woman; she lived to a great age and all through the war she continued the same occupation so far as the war would permit but her house was finally burned and her business was destroyed, and she retired to live with her daughter in the house which is now the rectory of St. Philips Episcopal Church, and ended there her long and useful life regretted by all but by none more than the children of Smithville to whom she supplied cakes which were so celebrated as to acquire the name of "Duffy Cakes." This steamship line was discontinued on the completion of the railroad, called The Wilmington & Manchester which carried all through passengers for southern ports or cities. As may be well imagined, this left Smithville aground upon the shoals, and what to do was a matter for serious consideration. How to get anywhere from Smithville was a difficulty not easily solved; there were few horses or vehicles of any kind in Smithville, but the river was there at any rate, and if you did not wish to go by land, and ride in a cart you could take a boat, of which there were plenty, and plenty of skillful boatmen to manage them; but neither of these modes of travel suited the public. Mr. Elijah Owen who kept an old fashioned house of entertainment in Smithville had two horses but no buggy; besides one of these horses was an ancient quadruped whose business it was to attend to the transportation of all persons who died to their last resting place, and his services might be required at any moment, and in consideration of these services, he was granted the freedom of the town, and was pastured in the streets of Smithville, from which place he did not wish to go. The other horse was, during the intervals between courts, mostly engaged in transporting people in the country and ploughing fields belonging to "Uncle Elijah." So the people sat down, and waited, and waited for the arrival of the Rev. Mr. Pickett, and his wife who traveled the circuit in a "one horse shay," and being a man of varied resources of entertaining the people they were always glad to see him approach. The Rev. Mr. Pickett was a man who preached the gospel strictly on Sundays and during the rest of the days of the week, he sat and smoked his pipe in peace, and left his parishioners to enjoy life in their own way. At this time the people of the churches, and their preachers had'nt [sic] gone into politics, or any of the side issues which at the present day perplex the minds of the people, and draw their attention away from sacred things; so when the time came, when this reverend gentleman was expected, the citizens who had been sitting on logs or in boats gazing out upon the broad Atlantic for ships to heave in sight turned their backs upon the river, and the ocean, and gazed out in the direction of the country anxiously awaiting his approach that they might grasp his friendly hand in their own, and bid him welcome. It may be well here to remark, that though they were mostly engaged in maritime pursuits they did not forget that there was a better country ahead of them to which sooner or later they must all travel, and they wanted to have the way pointed out to them so they would not be likely to get ashore or lost in any fog which might arise.

In the absence of steam communication it was found necessary to utilize the river as the best way for getting to Wilmington, so one or two enterprising men provided sailing packets on which they embarked and if the wind was fair they made good time to the city. If the wind was ahead however or a dead calm and they had to anchor it has come down to us by common report that they had a pretty good time on board; plenty to eat, and something also to drink which seemed to keep up their spirits while they waited for some body on board, to stick jack knives in the main mast, and whistle for the wind. These adventurous people always arrived in Wilmington Some-Time which was sufficient. Capt. Samuel Potter, and Capt. Samuel Price were captains in whom they could put implicit trust, and as they were not in a hurry they did not complain.

But the necessity of a better mode of travel between Wilmington, and Smithville, soon led to the establishment of a steamboat passenger line by Mr. A.H. Van Boklen the largest distiller of turpentine in the city of Wilmington.

He put on the line the steamer "Spray" greatly to the satisfaction of Wilmington, and Smithville, but her schedule was only for summer trade, and at the close of the summer season she was laid up, and soon afterward she was burned. This steamer was under the command of Capt. John B. Price, a Cape Fear pilot of marked ability, and well fitted for the business. She brought down all the summer residents, of whom there were now a great many, and her decks were crowded with passengers, and excursionists. It was about this time that the first tug boats ever on the Cape Fear River were put into service. One of these was the "Mariner" under command of Capt. John Davis, the other was the "Equator" under command of Jacob A.T. Price. These tug boats however, did not wish to carry passengers and only did so as a favor; so that the means provided for travellers was very unsatisfactory. They assisted greatly in the towing of vessels which was all [that] was wanted by the merchants of Wilmington. The time of their service on the Cape Fear River was very short as the war which shortly afterwards began captured nearly everything which floated upon the sea. The summer residents of Smithville did not however depend upon these tug boats as they came to Smithville for fun and enjoyment and did not care much whether they went to Wilmington or not until the season was over. They were planters along the Cape Fear river, and retired merchants of Wilmington, and they formed the most delightful society in Smithville for they believed in Smithville as a most delightful place of residence, and were interested in everything that was done and participated in all the amusements of the place. But we are now getting close upon a time when every amusement and every interest commercial or otherwise was to feel the dreadful shock of impending war, and go out of existence, leaving Smithville as lonesome and bereft of all pleasure as its worst enemies could desire. In the next chapter of these reminiscences I will go back, and give some account of what happened in more peaceful times.

CHAPTER THREE

During the ten years from 1850 to 1860, being cut off from daily communication with Wilmington, Smithville relapsed into a state of quietude which was first broken by the news that a company of United States troops had been ordered to Smithville. As this was expected to enliven the place to a great degree, and much interest was manifested to find out why soldiers had been ordered to occupy the place which was so far from anything war-like, that it might be called a "haven of rest." It was explained however, that in the adjoining state of South Carolina trouble was brewing on account of certain laws which had been passed by Congress which did not suit people in that state. Threats were made that they would not support or obey the law and consequently the Government thought that they would prepare for any emergency that might occur, and that it would be best to have troops within call, and that was the reason why these troops were sent to Smithville, under command of Major Ridgely (1852) and there were quite a number of young officers under his command which at once interested all the young people of both Smithville, and Wilmington, with the prospect that there would be much gaiety such as is usual at a military post in time of peace. The people of Smithville therefore resumed all those friendly relations which they had been accustomed to in former years when Col. Childs, Major Churchill had been stationed at Fort Johnson [sic]. In those days there was something more than friendly relations, as these relations ripened into marriage. During that time also the officers in command, initiated many improvements not only in the garrison grounds, but also in the town of Smithville. A beautiful double row of cedars was planted on the front, which in a few years grew into a shady walk, where the young people could promenade, and witness the military operations and drill and dress parade, to see which all the residence population gathered in the garrison. A friendly relation grew between the people, and the military. The officers all joined with the citizens of the town in their desire to have a church in Smithville, and a little Church was built which afterwards received the name of St. Philips Chapel, named after the old Church at Brunswick which was deserted and in ruins. The new Church was not organized until 1853, when a meeting of the parishioners was held and the following persons were elected vestryman, viz: John Hamlin Hill, Owen D. Holmes, Frederick J. Lord, Samuel Langdon, Dr. Walter G. Curtis, of which number Dr. John H. Hill, and Owen D. Holmes, were elected wardens, and Dr. Walter G. Curtis secretary and treasurer. Services were occasionally held by the Rev. Dr. Draine of St. James Parish, Wilmington, and lay reading by Dr. Hill, and Samuel Langdon. This Church was consecrated by the Rt. Rev. Thomas Atkinson, Bishop of North Carolina.

The Company of United States troops was ordered away in 1852, and two companies of the third Artillery took their place under command of Capt. J.P. McCown. The second company was under command of Capt. Getty, who afterwards was promoted to the rank of Major Genl. in the Federal service and served with distinction during the entire civil war. Capt. McCown resigned from the Federal service, and so soon as war was declared was appointed Major Genl. in the Confederate service. The difficulties which threatened in North Carolina having been amicably adjusted, the two companies under the command of Capt. McCown were ordered away, leaving Fort Johnston in charge of ordinance Sergt. John Belger. The troops were ordered away greatly to the sorrow of the people of Wilmington, and Smithville who had one and all endeared themselves to the people. During their stay however Capt. John A. Brown had become engaged to Miss Mildred Holmes, and they were shortly after married.

The next year after these companies of the army left Fort Johnston a large force of officers and civilians employed by the United States Coast Survey under command of Capt. John N. Maffatt were ordered to make a survey at the mouth of the Cape Fear river; then the festivities which had been interrupted were recommenced, Capt. Maffat being the chief promoter, and leader in all social enterprises as well as commander of the surveying force at the mouth of the Cape Fear. The principal social event was the formation of a troupe of private theatricals, the company comprising nearly all the officers and civilians engaged in the survey together with all the society people of Smithville who felt themselves competent to appear upon the stage; and many plays were acted greatly to the satisfaction, and amusement of their audiences; the barrack building on the Garrison ground being fitted up as a theater.

In performance of these plays Capt. Maffatt was easily the most brilliant star. In the theatrical company were Capt. Charles Bolles, Lieut A.C. Ryan of the U.S. Navy, who was elected by Genl. Benj. F. Butler to command the celebrated powder ship which was expected to blow up Fort Fisher, and drive its garrison in terror into the woods and adjoining swamps, but none of these dire results happened. The summer of 1854 passed away in Smithville and much happiness prevailed in town. The young men of the Coast Survey were unable to resist the attractions of the young ladies who were present that summer, and Capt. Charles Bolles was soon after married to Miss Eliza Walker of Wilmington. Mr. Gregory of coast survey married Miss Sallie Baker also of Wilmington. All went happily and no one present at any of these festive occasions could, by the widest stretch of the imagination ever have believed that the roar of hostile cannon would ever disturb the serenity which pervaded society in quiet Smithville, but which they were forced to hear only a few short years later.

It seems proper at this point of the story which is being related to say that very few of the actors and actresses, and lookers on upon these festivities are now alive to see this imperfect recital of the doings of our younger days. Many of the officers of the Army, and Navy whose homes are herein mentioned acquired great distinction by their deeds of valor in the civil war which soon began. All that happened during the few years between 1852 and 1856 has been a digression from the story of Smithville; but as inhabitants and residents were connected with these historical events it has been deemed proper to insert them here.

We will now return to Smithville proper, and describe some of the things which happened during that time. But before I proceed, let me say that every thing which has hitherto happened has been peaceful and calls to my mind the beautiful words of the poet;

> "Oh! love peace with beauty crowned,
> Oh! lovely, lovely peace.
> Come shed thy blessings all abroad,
> And crown the hills with flocks and herds,
> Let valleys shine with waving corn."

This is peace, and I hesitate to chronicle the things which must come after. They are many, and numerous, and dreadful to contemplate. War, pestilence, and almost famine are close at hand and yet the people who had lived so long in peace do not, and cannot appreciate it. I have to chronicle Smithville as a military camp and confusion worse confounded every where. Far worse than war pestilence, and famine was the period called "Reconstruction." That period, which is some years from the present writing I shall postpone until I can speak of certain other peaceful times. As almost every one of the actors in the proceeding pages have gone to their rest some by means of the war some by the natural course of age, others by disease which swept them away as if a tempest had swept over the land. I have not alluded to many persons, except those who had had a high character and bore a prominent part in the service of their country and their memory will not be forgotten.

CHAPTER FOUR

We will now return to our reminiscences of Smithville proper and will here say, that Smithville is not Smithville when invaded by people having interests foreign to repose. Not that Smithville is not interested in outside affairs but they are as clouds which obscure the sun for a moment then pass by. "Sufficient unto the day is the evil thereof" is a motto which might well be inscribed upon the banners of this ancient town.

There were interesting scenes often happening which partially changed the even tenor of her way. There were the Courts of law, and the Magistrates Courts which excited great interest, but this interest was temporary in its character. There were four terms of the Courts of law each year; two for the Superior Courts of Law, and two Courts held by the Justices of the Peace of the county, in which county affairs were mostly dealt with. The holding of these Courts, and the transaction of their business was solely in the hands of the white people of the state; there were no negroes present because they had no business in any court; they were the wards of the white population who attended to their needs, their interests, with as much care, and fidelity as they did their own. There were no criminals among the negro population; their place of business was at home, and their work was in the fields, in workshops sometime and the family residence of their owners; they were a quiet, and happy people having plenty to eat, clothes to wear, and a doctor to administer to their ailments which were very few, and simple. If they committed any deeds which were contrary to the rules, and regulations of their home life, they were punished with great moderation, for they were a part of the family and their lives and their good health was essential to the prosperity of the home which was so valuable to them; they had no responsibility except responsibilities to work, and perform their duty and it was a rare thing for one of them to be over-burdened by excessive labor. Indeed it was not required of them that they should put forth all their energies because it was seldom necessary that they should do so. Most of them were docile, polite, and devoted to the interest of their home. Of what use was it to them to commit murder, or burglary or arsons or assaults with intent to kill? It was not their nature or interest to commit such offenses, and therefore they were not required to go to court except as carriage drivers, or body servants to their masters. It follows therefore as a matter of course, that the white people went to court for various reasons such as pleased them. Some had business in the courts, and were jurors, and witnesses and officers of the court; but many went for the mere pleasure of meeting their friends, and acquaintances from distant parts of the County. A good many of the younger men went for the purpose of showing off their fine horses, and their skillful horsemanship; and always they were ready for a horse trade. At times when elections were going on, they went to hear the public speaking, and to post themselves on the issues of the day. Up to 1861 they were divided into two parties only, which were Whigs and Democrats. Both of these parties were composed of men of the highest respectability, and they loved to talk to each other of the respective merits of their candidates. The principles also of these two parties were respectable, and so much as they believed to be for the interest of their common county which they loved with great devotion and there were no side issues attached to principles of either party. These side issues were left to the people to talk over in their homes and neighborhood, so each man could decide what he thought was best, and keeping them out of national politics and where they could do no harm. In former years which was a long time ago, the Judges were attended to the Court House by the Sheriff with a drawn sword in his hand. On his approach, and entrance into the court room, a great hush settled upon the audience who desired to show their respect for law, and order. The trials were conducted with great dignity on the part of the Judge, and strict attention to the evidence on the part of the jury, and decisions of the Court were usually just, so that appeals to the Supreme Court were not as common as at present. Mr. John Brown, a gentleman of great respectability and a long resident in Smithville was clerk of this court and being so quiet and inoffensive in his manners, it seemed very hard that in the later years of his life, when confusion worse confounded prevailed everywhere, that he should have been so pressed with trials which could have killed many a man before those trials were finished. In 1862 an epidemic of yellow fever started in Wilmington, the disease having been brought thither by a blockade steamer. It raged with extreme virulence in that city, and caused the death of a large portion of its inhabitants, including many of its most distinguished citizens. All who could, escape from the city, and went where they could find places to live. A large number of these refugees came to Smithville, and brought the disease with them. Robt. W. Brown, a son of Mr. John Brown, who had sailed to Nassau in his schooner, contracted fever in Nassau, and died there. About this time when Mr. Robt. Brown died in Nassau, the news was brought home, that Capt John B. Price had also died and both these gentlemen were buried in a foreign soil. Mr. Brown's next succeeding misfortune was the death of his daughter Mrs. R. G. Rankin, and his daughter-in-law Mrs. Robt. W. Brown both of whom contracted the disease from a trunk containing the clothing of Capt. Robt. Brown which was sent home from Nassau. The disease then spread to the house of Mr. Phillip Prioleau, whose wife, the daughter of Mr. John Brown, together with two of her sons, Thomas and John Prioleau died in the midst of the confusion which reigned in the town of Smithville, and the universal terror which prevailed, lest other victims might fall in quick succession and while Mr. L. McGinney, Mr. Brown's son-in-law, was lying sick almost to death in the family residence of Mr. Brown, and there seemed none to help or nurse the sick, a fire broke out in an adjoining house belonging to Dr. S.B. Everett. Soon the fire spread to Mr. Brown's house, and these fine residences were all burnt to the ground. Mr. McGinney was carried out of the house while it was burning in almost a dying condition, but he afterwards recovered; leaving the old people, Mr. and Mrs. Brown, and Miss Valeria, their daughter destitute upon the streets of Smithville and while death, and fire was destroying all this valuable property in Smithville, many of his negroes escaped to the blockade steamers which lay outside the bar.

As before mentioned there were two Superior Courts, and two County or Majistrates [sic] courts each year; during the session of these latter courts, the bench was occupied by the principal justices of the peace of Brunswick County from which body Mr. Danl. L. Russell, Sr. was Chairman, and Saml. Langdon, clerk of the said court. Mr. Russell was a man of acknowledged ability as presiding majistrate, and otherwise, and was re-elected year after year for many years. While Mr. Saml. Langdon lived he retained his office of clerk, and was in fact, the chief adviser of the court, the lawyers and the people, who depended upon him for assistance in every trouble they might have in their affairs. Mr. Langdon was par excellence friend to the people whom he served with the utmost geniality, and interest always without compensation; and it was thought by the people that he so much belonged to them and would serve them cheerfully even if he had to do so without food. The majistrate's courts were conducted with dignity, and under the same conditions as regarded race and color, as prevailed in the Superior Courts. This state of affairs, public, and private prevailed until the war begun in 1861. Smithville always quiet, and serene maintained its character every summer being filled with its summer residents who were the planters from the Cape Fear River, and many of the principle citizens of Wilmington and the utmost friendliness prevailed between the summer residents and those who resided in Smithville.

The business of the town, if business it had, was the piloting of vessels, and this was of course conducted upon the waters of the Cape Fear. The business of pilots was a great interest to the public who witnessed their operations with the greatest attention, because it was certainly a magnificent panorama to look at when twenty or thirty vessels appeared off the bar and were brought in under full sail and passed in front of the town in full view of all its inhabitants, and when they had taken in their cargoes in Wilmington, and passed again out so sea, the view was equally inspiring.

· CHAPTER FIVE .

Many other things had happened during this period, of which I have written in this chapter, which cast a gloom upon the community. Mr. Richard Langdon, the father of Mr.Samuel Langdon, died, and Mrs. Langdon after a few years, followed her husband to the grave. Mr. Langdon was a merchant much esteemed in Smithville, and he had been contemporary with Governor Benjamin Smith, who passed the last years of his life in Smithville, and for whom the town derived its name he having donated the land upon which the town was laid out.

He had been a benefactor not only to the town of Smithville, but had also given a large tract of land to the University of North Carolina. His residence was upon the spot which was to be occupied by another Governor of the state besides himself, viz; Gov. Dudley. This residence was situated at the corner of Bay, and Potts Sts., where the Hotel Brunswick now stands. The death of Gov. Smith was a sad one to all who had known him for his generosity and public spirit. The Memorial Hall at the University of North Carolina was built as a tribute to the memory of his life, and character.

The old home of Mr. Richard Langdon was now occupied by his son Mr. Samuel Langdon, who to the citizens of Smithville was a guide, philosopher, and friend; he married Miss McRae of Fayetteville, a sister of the Hon. Jas. C. McRae, now dean of the law Faculty of the University. The death of Mrs. Samuel Langdon was an event which effected the people of Smithville with deep regret, for she was a woman of great intelligence, kind and friendly to all who knew her. Mr. and Mrs. Samuel Langdon lived very happily together in the old family residence which was a house of the oldest style of architecture, of which there are now no specimens left in the town of Smithville. As might have been expected Mr. Langdon did not live very long after the loss of his lovely wife, and great was the sorrow of the community over his death which seemed untimely. He was a man of stalwart form such as ought have resisted the approach of the great reaper, Death. Mr. Samuel Langdon came of a family distinguished for learning and in several walks of life. He was descended from Dr. Samuel Langdon who was born in Boston, Mass., 1722 and was settled over the old

16

North Church of historic fame. Paul Revere started from that point on his famous ride. His pastorate lasted twenty nine years when he resigned to accept the Chaplaincy of troops under Sir William Pepperell, going with them on the famous expedition to Louisburg. Later he was elected president of Harvard college, and held this position for six years. In 1780 he returned to the pulpit and was settled over the Parish Church in Hampton Falls. He died in 1787, still pastor of his church then a prominent organization covering a large territory in the southeastern part of New Hampshire. The Society of The Daughters of The American Revolution proposed to erect a monument over his grave in the old Parish graveyard at Hampton Falls, and have probably done so. Two of his sons emigrated to North Carolina. One settled in Wilmington, and the other, Mr. Richard Langdon settled in Smithville, and died there a few years before the date of the beginning of this record, leaving two children, viz; Samuel Langdon and one daughter who married Col. S.L. Fremont, who was the son of L. Sewell Fish of New Hampshire; the same family as the Hamilton Fish of New York, who are people of influence and position. He received the appointment, and entered West Point Military Academy. After graduating he decided to change his name from Fish to Fremont, which was done through an act of the Legislature. After graduation at West Point he served in the U.S. army. For several years he, with his family were on board the troopship San Francisco which was wrecked off the Atlantic coast on her way to the Isthmus. Miss Emeline Everett, daughter of Dr. S. B. Everett, who married Maj. Taylor, who was also on board the steamship was lost with her husband, but Col. Fremont, and family were saved and came home to Smithville from which place he resigned as officer of the U.S. Army.

Many other officers who suffered great destruction in the civil war, resided in Smithville at different times during this period, among whom may be mentioned Capt. D. P. Woodbury afterwards General, and commanded the Engineer force which brought the Federal Army in safety through the swamps of the Chicahominy to the banks of the James river where one of the greatest battles of the war was fought. Captain Whiting, afterwards Major General in the Confederate Army was stationed at Fort Johnson [sic] in Smithville, a considerable time.

He married Miss Kate Walker daughter of Major John Walker of Wilmington.

Mr. Thomas D. Meares, well known and remembered in Brunswick county, and who represented the county in the North Carolina Legislature, who owned a large rice plantation which now belongs to the Navassa Guano Co. made Smithville his summer home, and built a fine residence on the corner of Bay and Potts sts. where he brought his family to live and no doubt expected to spend the last years of his life in ease and comfort, but who was deprived of that pleasure by the war, which wrecked his fortune. He left a large family of children. He married Miss Jane Iredell, the daughter of Judge Iredell, a man distinguished in the state of North Carolina for his learning. Among his children we take the liberty of mentioning Iredell Meares Esq. who became a lawyer, and keeps up the family name for learning and distinction.

But there were many others who ought to be mentioned and whose names ought not to be forgotten. Mr. Thos. McHenny, Frederick J. Lord, Philip Prioleau, Dr. John H. Hill, Owen D. Holmes, Dr. Fred Hill, Thos. Cowan, and Henry N. Howard, were all rice planters from the Cape Fear river, men of education and refinement who spent their summers in Smithville, and were friends of that town to the very last. Mr. Robt. W. Brown also had a fine residence in Smithville, and after a long life as a commission merchant in Wilmington, he loved to spend his summers in ease and tranquility. These gentlemen have all passed over the river, and are forever at rest from their labors, and they leave behind them a record of being Southern gentlemen than which there can be no higher reputation to be desired. There were many others scattered through the county who never lived in Smithville, but they were well known to all its inhabitants as good citizens, and men of the highest worth; many of them sat in the county Board of Magistrates, making the county court of Brunswick the equal of any in the state of North Carolina.

But the clouds that had been gathering over the country, and constantly thickening, and casting over the whole country a shadow of impending danger were now fast coming to an issue. All kinds of business ceased, all improvements ceased, and all men stood in doubt of what was to come. They did not know anything about war for they had lived in peace.

The two great parties which had hitherto governed the country were the Whig, and Democratic parties and the people generally believed they were wise and patriotic, and well fitted to take the lead in whatever events were to follow, and those events did follow thick and fast, and it was war which followed, and all good citizens believed it was their duty to defend their country, and more especially their native state.

There were no vessels coming in from the north and most of those which were already here were loading, and departing as fast as possible. Even the small vessels which ran up the creeks and inlets found little business awaiting them at the landing. The distilleries at Wilmington ceased their operations and the saw mills only supplied the local demand for lumber. The works of improvement upon the river ceased and there was nothing to do but to wait.

CHAPTER SIX

From the earliest times when the site of Wilmington was selected, it was seen that no great commercial business could be successfully carried on, unless improvements could be made in the depth of water in the river below Wilmington. It was full of shoals, and only vessels of light draft could be used and these could not be relied upon for ocean navigation, and shipment of cargoes to New York, and other northern cities.

The value of the pine tree had been discovered both for lumber, and naval stores. The lumber trade was mostly carried on with the West Indies, and the naval store trade with domestic ports north, and it was necessary that larger vessels be used and vessels of deeper draft; consequently this subject was investigated by civilian engineers who were supposed to have some knowledge of such matters, and

19

opinions were given freely as to what should be done. It was at first considered that the river ought to improve itself with some help by the engineer's project. The state made some small appropriations, and jetties were constructed below Wilmington in order to concentrate the force of the tide in the channel which would become deeper by the force of the water. But this produced but small effect. It was found that the river was full of cypress stumps, and logs, showing that at this locality there had once been extensive cypress swamps. To clear out these obstructions therefore must first be accomplished, and this required heavier machinery than the state or city could furnish. Heavy dredging boats had not at this time been invented nor was the capital at hand to operate such machinery, consequently the idea was suggested that this work must be done by the general government. Therefore Congress was applied to [to] make an appropriation, and send engineers of ability to execute the work. The work did not progress rapidly for some years, but there were men of influence, and ability in Wilmington and public meeting[s] were held and committees appointed to go to Washington and represent the state of affairs to Congress, and the United States Engineers. By this means appropriations were made, and engineers dispatched to survey the river and make report of their proceedings.

Mr. Henry Nutt, a merchant of Wilmington, and a man full of enterprise was able to see what the future of Wilmington might be if the river was opened. Mr. Nutt was a distiller of turpentine, and had large amounts of the product on the pine tree to be shipped, and the business was growing in magnitude, and its influence felt upon the business of the country. But even the engineers of the United States had little or no experience in these matters and the improvements lagged, lagged. After repeated trials, many different plans resulting in little benefit to navigation, it was determined that the key to the position was the filling up of the New Inlet, and the consequence was the filling up of that inlet, and the consequent diverting the whole force of that tide into one channel, which would be down the river, and out of the bar at the mouth of the river.

The New Inlet was a large opening into the ocean made by a severe storm over a hundred years ago. About half the water of the river on ebb tide went out by way of this channel, and the incoming tide stopped the currents above the New Inlet, and caused it to deposit shoals in many places. It was seen to be a very huge and difficult task to stop up this channel and there were several other openings near the Inlet which were nearly as bad and had to be stopped. This was accomplished largely by bags filled with sand, which were dumped into these channels, and a beginning, made to stop up the New Inlet by means of cribs of timber which were loaded with stone.

"But man proposes, and God disposes," and a great storm arose which swept away everything in its path, and all the attempts of improvement came to naught; besides this, dark war clouds arose and prevented all further efforts for the time being.

The large stock of naval stores which lay upon the wharves in Wilmington must be disposed of and transported to market with all possible speed. Vessels were loaded with as much dispatch as possible, and a great number of other vessels were sent to the port of Wilmington to load with naval stores for northern markets, and thus the stock which had accumulated was disposed of before war had actually been declared. The laborers in the forests were called to their homes, and they brought their tools with them. The distilleries ceased operating and the stock in market lessened with great rapidity; and when the war actually opened there were but very few vessels on the ocean bound for New York.

All business came to a standstill waiting to see what was going to happen. The pilots who had brought these vessels down the river and out to sea, came to their homes and also waited. Smithville itself assumed a condition of utter quiet, and the visitors who usually came to spend the summer remained at their homes. Nothing was talked of among the people but the state of political affairs, and its probable effect upon the country; and this condition continued until the opening of the year of 1861 when war actually began in the state of South Carolina, and Fort Sumter in the harbor of Charleston was summoned to surrender. Ships loaded with provisions and war supplies were ordered by the Government to Charleston, and when they arrived they were fired upon from batteries commanding the bar, and these vessels being only transports without armament of any kind on board turned around, and returned to the northern ports from whence they came. The garrison at Fort Sumter refusing to surrender, fire was opened upon the fort from many batteries in the vicinity, and after a terrible bombardment lasting a few days, the garrison which consisted of only a few soldiers under Major Anderson, was forced to surrender and the United States flag was hauled down. The effect in the town of Smithville was very great; all citizens were in a state of the greatest excitement to hear the news, and when the result was reported to them they knew that war had actually begun, and that their business was changed from the arts of peace to those of war with all its attendant horrors. War was something new to the quiet citizens of Smithville, and the matter was discussed by all the people including men, women, and children. There were visitors in Smithville whose homes were in the north, and they immediately packed their trunks and started upon what they knew to be a perilous journey. The Government however, did not interfere with travelers of this description and they were given permits to pass the lines, and go to their homes in the north. The citizens of Brunswick county came in from all quarters to find out the news, and returned to distribute it, and to carry gloom to the homes of every citizen.

CHAPTER SEVEN

On a bright morning in the month of May 1861, the sun rose clear and beautiful, and the ocean at New Inlet exhibited its display of fireworks in the shape of dancing waves which greeted the rising sun. Nature was happy at any rate and apparently wished everyone else to be happy. The citizens of Smithville walked about the streets a little, and then sat down to talk and to wait. About noon a sloop was seen approaching from up the river; but most of the citizens who watched and waited upon the shore were pilots who did not take much interest in anything but large ships and so they did not manifest any interest in the vessel; but the small boy had put in his appearance on the wharf, and it was seen that they were greatly excited about what was to happen, and they cried out with one voice, "the soldiers have come." And so they had, for presently the tap of drum was heard and the soldiers landed, and forming ranks, marched up the street and through the garrison gate to the officer's quarters which seemed to be deserted. They formed a line in front of the door and at the command of their Captain, ordered arms and then stood at rest. Then the Captain advanced to meet the soldier who stood at the entrance, informed him that they had come to take possession of the Government property, and asked him to surrender. This officer was Ord. Sergt. James T. Riley of the U.S. Ord. Corps. Sergt. Riley was not a man to surrender anything without good reasons for so doing. He looked around him and saw a superior force against which he could not contend, and he therefore asked the attacking force of soldiers what they proposed to do, and they informed him that they wanted the keys of the guard house, and the ordnance storehouse. Having given up the keys, he was told that he could continue to live in the house until further orders from the Governor of North Carolina. Sentinels were then detailed to guard the place, and give due notice of the approach of any hostile force which seemed able or desirous of disputing the possession of the property; and so ended the first battle of war in Smithville. The troops were then assembled and marched back to their vessel which was lying at the wharf. They then set sail for Fort Caswell at which place they landed and marched to the Fort where Ord. Sergt. Dardankiller was in command. He also was summoned to surrender the fort and all property therein, which he did, seeing he could not help himself; therefore the troops marched into the fort and took possession, the officer disposing his forces upon the parapets, and at the gates of the fortress after which the military forces were dismissed to await events, with instructions to be ready for action at the first alarm.

But no alarm followed and they settled themselves down to get as much ease as they could, which was mighty little. On inspection the fort was found to be dilapidated and almost unfit for human habitation. There were no guns mounted which could be fired, the moat was nearly filled with sand and mud, and there was not a room in the fort finished of furnished; mosquitoes were the only energetical objects that made an appearance. To the troops who had performed this service for their country, there did not seem to be any of the pomp or circumstance of "glorious war;" but it was necessary to keep up some form of military display and the sentinels posted upon the walls were ordered to give immediate notice of the approach of any hostile ships which were seen to enter the harbor. None came however and after waiting a few days a liner steamer was seen approaching which they found to be the bearer of dispatches to the effect that the troops occupying Fort Johnston and Fort Caswell should evacuate those places and return immediately to Wilmington where they were to disperse and return to their homes. It was explained that North Carolina had not yet seceded from the Union, and until she had done so the United States were the rightful possessors of all such property.

The inhabitants of Smithville looked at each other and wondered. They had not thought that the war would end so soon, without the loss of a single man. But North Carolina soon after seceded from the Union and orders were given by the Governor, that troops designated for the service should take possession of the Government property within the limits of North Carolina. When this was done all could see that the war had actually begun for troops in sufficient numbers came and took possession of the property and held it against all invaders for four years until the close of the war. While this was going on however the inhabitants of Smithville who were not liable to military service and were therefore non-combatants met together on the street corners, and elsewhere and had much serious and wise conversation on the condition of affairs in the town of Smithville. They saw that every man liable to military service would be summoned to take the field and help fight the battles of his country. They saw also that civil law had also ceased to operate and that there might be much disorder among and between the soldiers and the citizens who were about to occupy the place. They discussed the situation as regarded the women and children of the place who might be unprotected. They felt that the little property that they possessed might be very insecure since they had heard that the Confederate soldier believed that one of the functions of his position was to defend women and children and that therefore anything lying around they had a right to take without leave or license, also without compensation to the owners. They actually did take such fences as they saw would be convenient for fire wood. They also discovered a turpentine distillery in the yard of which there was about four hundred barrels of rosin; they thought it very convenient to make fires with; they therefore took, and burnt up the whole of it as they wanted it. The full worth of this rosin was about two or three thousand dollars. Much confusion prevailed at first and the old citizens of the town proposed the establishment of the "home guard" for the protection of their home interests. Consequently a public meeting was called to meet at the court house, and after much discussion an organization was formed. Mr. John Bell was elected Captain, his chief qualifications being that he was good natured and not likely to enforce any military discipline whatever. Much wisdom was apparent in the proceeding of the conversation of these ancient gentlemen. They therefore proposed to the Captain a great number of things heretofore unheard of in any military organization; the principal one being that as they were liable to become fatigued by the exertion of marching and inquiring of the citizens "if they were well" and listening to their replies that "they were not to say well, that they had a mighty hurting in their heads and a misery in their backs" which being duly reported to Captain Bell he would reply by saying that "he was sorry for their infirmities but that Mustang liniment was a good thing to rub on the aching places and that a small quantity of Plantation Bitters taken internally would finish the cure." Captain Bell issued orders then that they should all meet for drill the next morning and one member of the force proposed to the Captain that the soldiers of the "home guard" should be required to bring camp stools with them so that when they were tired they could sit down and rest. Captain Bell then gave the order of "attention" and put them through the various drills marching around the town and it was observed that when one of the company got opposite to his own home he left the ranks and was no more seen. The "home guard" being thus weakened so that they could not face any kind of an enemy, it was moved and seconded by one of the members that the "home guard" be now discontinued, to which motion Captain Bell remarked that he "thought so too" and the motion being unanimously carried thus ended the famous "home guard."

It may here be mentioned that Ord. Sergt. Jas. T. Riley resigned his position in the Ord. Corps of the United States Army and as soon as his resignation was accepted he enlisted in the Artillery service of the Confederate Army. He was soon promoted to the rank of Major in which position he served through the war with great gallantry distinguishing himself in many of the hard fought battles of the war. Sergt. Dardankiller however as soon as he could procure transportation returned to the north and nothing further was ever heard from him.

CHAPTER EIGHT

As has been related in previous chapters, the procession of events now continued with increasing rapidity. Day by day the condition of affairs in Smithville was different from what it had been the day before. Orders were issued by the Governor of the state that all able bodied men that were liable to do military duty must immediately report to the nearest enrolling officer for the purpose of being attached to some military company or regiment. By this order Smithville was deprived of a large number of its male citizens, and the streets of the town began to assume a look entirely foreign to its hitherto quiet, and peaceful aspect; for as soon as the Smithville contingent had left, their place was filled with whole companies of soldiers from other counties and towns of the state. The first company that arrived was the Rowan Rifle Guards, commanded by Captain Hamilton Jones. The next company was the Duplin Guards under Capt. Claude Denson. These two companies brought with them complete camp equipage, and they pitched their camp alongside the brick walk in the Garrison and in the shade of the beautiful cedars which had been planted many years ago by Col. Churchill of the United States Army, at a time when all were at peace, and nobody expected that this happy and prosperous government would ever be otherwise than of peace. Then followed in quick succession two companies from Cabarrus county which were the "Cabarrus Black Boys" under Capt,— One of these companies took up their quarters in the barracks. The "Black Boys" had their quarters in the hospital building which the United States had erected. Other companies followed in quick succession. Two companies from Columbus county who found quarters in the Garrison enclosure. Other companies who found the Garrison full were quartered on the town. Company G. 20th N.C. Garland's Brigade was from Brunswick county, and quartered on Franklin Square, under Capt. John H. Brooks, 1st Lieut. Oliver E. Mercer, 2nd Lieut. Thos. C. Fulwood. Company C. 30th N.C. Anderson's Brigade, Capt. Green, 1st Lieut. D. C. Allen, 2nd Lieut. S. P. Tharp from North West. D. L. Russell's company of artillery, and Capt. John D. Taylor's company were ordered to Fort Caswell for duty. There were also two companies from Sampson county who were sent to Smithville for drill. Smithville was now full of soldiers, and the town presented the appearance of a military camp. Patrols were ordered to patrol the streets, and sentinels at the corners of the streets, and the work of drilling commenced. The sound of "hep, hep," was continual and was the only music except that of the drum. These companies being detached companies, were many of them from time to time ordered away to join regiments in other parts of the state.

Steamboats such as were then on the Cape Fear river—most of them hardly fit for service—were passing to and from Smithville to Wilmington bringing recruits, Commissary and Quartermaster's stores. The wives and children of soldiers in the camp who came to see their husbands and sweethearts before the final parting which was not expected to happen for all these soldiers were needed to help fight the battles of the Confederacy to Virginia. It seems proper to say at this point that the citizens parted with these soldier boys with considerable regret for they were sober and stalwart men not addicted to strong drink or the vices which at the present day of advanced civilization require acts of Legislature to keep them within the bounds of propriety. Prohibition as a moral agent had not been invented at that time and in reality it was not required. Every Soldier ate and drank what he wanted and wore such clothes as he could get. Now the soldiers having departed it was felt that Smithville was a lonely spot on the earth's surface. But as if for the purpose of enlivening matters somewhat great ships were discovered on the ocean approaching the Cape Fear bar and five or six of them dropped their anchors. This was the blockading fleet which had been sent by the United States to shut up the door of the Cape Fear and prevent either ingress or egress. To the eyes of a pilot this fleet of great ships was a glorious sight to look upon as they had not seen any ships for a long time. They thought of the time which had passed when the river was full of ships waiting [for] a pilot and they hoped for a time when peace should arrive and commerce be re-established. They did not have to wait long however before they were notified by the Confederate Government to hold themselves in readiness to carry out such vessels as might be ready to run the blockade. This blockade running business had already begun and one steamship, "The Kate" commanded by Captain Tom Lockwood a native of Smithville, a skillful and daring officer had attempted to bring her into port, and had been fired upon by the blockaders, and injured to such an extent that she sank inside the river in spite of all effort to keep her afloat. It was understood there were many other steamers loading in Nassau and preparing to try the perilous experiment of running in the port through the blockade. They found it easier to get in than they expected and most of them made the voyage a success although they were fired upon. As fast as they got ready to go out again a pilot was assigned to each vessel and notified when he might be wanted. Thus the pilots got again into business and were of great service to the Confederacy.

The army in the field required more supplies than the country could produce and they had to be imported. Vast quantities of arms and ammunitions, clothing, shoes and food were required to support the army in Virginia and it required the genius of men having great political and commercial activity. Fortunate was it for the North Carolina troops that so great a man as Zebulon B. Vance was governor of North Carolina. His patriotism and his sympathies were aroused to that extend that he devoted his entire time to furnishing through the blockade, supplies for North Carolina soldiers. Without the supplies furnished by the aid of Governor Vance a large part of the army in Virginia would have found themselves destitute. But we cannot follow the fortunes of the army in the field as those of the Southern people who had to remain at home soon found themselves in the presence of an enemy more powerful and more to be dreaded than the army in the field. Late in the summer of 1862 a blockade running steamer entered the port of Wilmington. There were cases of sickness on board the steamer and Mr. Fanning, Health Officer of the port had been driven from the vessel which required sanitary inspection, with indignity. Physicians were summoned to see the sick on board this steamer and though they suspected the nature of the disease they did not proclaim it to be Yellow fever to the public for several days. Then it was too late for the disease had penetrated to various parts of the city and soon became epidemic. The population of the city were terror stricken and they made every effort to escape to any place to where they could find refuge. Before they could escape, people were beginning to die and were stricken down so they could not leave. A considerable number of refugees however, came to Smithville where they occupied every available house. They brought the fever with them and many of these refugees died. But few of the permanent residents of Smithville contracted the disease and most of these recovered except the family of Mr. John Brown which has been heretofore narrated. During the prevalence of Yellow fever in Smithville nearly all the troops were ordered to leave the town and camp outside in the forest and there to await orders.

CHAPTER NINE

It is worthy of notice that Smithville though often exposed in years gone by did not contract yellow fever even though brought in contact with those who had the disease. Capt. Isaac B. Smith commanding the line steamer "C. Vanderbilt" contracted the disease in Charleston while it was raging in the city in great intensity in 1852. He was brought directly to his own home in Smithville and after being sick for several days, under the medical care of Doctor S. B. Everett, an old physician of great experience, he died in the midst of his large family who were constantly in attendance upon him. He was buried from his home. A large attendance of the people of Smithville were at his funeral. No one contracted the disease from him. There was another case which happened before this time, of a pilot or a sea captain who also contracted the disease in Charleston and was brought home to Smithville where he died without communicating the disease to anyone. There was still another case of a seaman from one of the steamers of the U.S. Coast Survey who died in the Garrison in the midst of a great number of his fellow seamen. A physician in the Confederate service went to Wilmington and stayed a couple of days and came back to Smithville where he died in a day or two with the most virulent case of yellow fever; he died in [the] most thickly populated part of the town but no one took the disease from him. Added to these examples the terrible misfortunes which happened to Mr. John Brown's family during which so many of them died were directly traceable to the clothes of his son Robt. W. Brown which were sent home from Nassau and those who handled these clothing contracted the disease and died but no case occurred outside his immediate family; so that it may be reasonably considered that Smithville possesses considerable immunity from yellow fever. The immigration from Wilmington soon ceased, there being no more quarters obtainable. Although the disease lasted in Smithville more than a month there were not more than two or three cases in the town, one of whom died and the other two recovered. It was some time before it was considered safe for the refugees to go back to their homes in Wilmington. In that city many hundreds died and the city being almost depopulated it was a common sight to see the dead carried to their last resting place in common pine boxes hauled by drays with few or no mourners attending the ceremony and no clergyman to say a prayer over these graves. This was in the year

1862. But in the natural course of events the disease declined as cold weather set in and frost occurred. Anxiously did the people of Smithville and Wilmington look for the first frost but no frost came until the 20th November which was a month later than the usual time when the disease became almost extinct.

Affairs now began to assume their natural aspect, and there was nothing to excite special notice except the roaring of the great guns from the blockading vessels, and it was facetiously remarked that it was intended to strike terror to the hearts of the "rebels" as there seemed nothing else to shoot at. Blockade running continued to increase, and the pilots were one by one notified to come to Wilmington and take charge of vessels which were loaded and ready to sail on the first dark night which should occur. The citizens of Smithville watched these matters with the greatest interest, and once in a while a great cannonading was heard at sea, and dense clouds of smoke issued from the funnels of the blockaders. There was nothing to do however but to wait for news, and it was very seldom that any reached Smithville until the steamers returned from another voyage. Once in a while news came to friends of the pilots, that one of their number had been captured; this meant generally they would not return until the end of the war. It was a great event in the history of blockade navigation when a vessel was attacked coming into port and was forced to run ashore to save the lives of the crew. Then a great excitement prevailed to get to the steamer ashore, and save all that could be saved; this kind of salvage was indulged in by soldiers at the forts, and by everybody that could get a boat to get alongside. This was a safe proceeding when a blockade steamer had gone ashore on the beach, because they were out of range of the enemies' cannon. There was a great deal of plunder saved which was of great use to everybody in vicinity of the wreck. Articles such as medical stores of all kinds, the most important of which was quinine, and Smithville did not suffer during the whole course of war for lack of that valuable drug.

Much clothing, including shoes and blankets for the soldiers use and sometimes large quantities of bacon, which was a valuable food for everybody. Chickery in hogsheads was also found and used by the people making them think that they were drinking coffee. A great many valuable boxes of surgical instruments were saved, but they were apt to be somewhat damaged by salt water. The steamer "Modern Greece" is an example of one of these ships, which went on the beach, under the guns of Fort Fisher. The steamer "Ella," whose bones project above the waters of "Bald Head" was a total loss.

There was very little else doing in Smithville except the welcoming home of an occasional pilot, or bidding farewell to some other one who was about to leave. The citizens who, during the last year, had been burning tallow, into which a wick of indifferent length was dipped, then wound upon a stick and then unwound, were eminently pleased when a pilot would bring home a kerosene lamp, and a gallon of kerosene, and these valuable articles were introduced first by Capt. Thomas M. Thompson. This running of the blockade was a most interesting and exciting business, and it continued to the very night when Fort Fisher was captured. Two blockade steamers came in on that eventful night when the great fleet off Fort Fisher was celebrating their victory by illuminations and fireworks of every description. There were two steamers that came in on this night commanded by Capt. Maffett, and sending a boat ashore and finding that Fort Fisher had been captured, he weighed anchor, went immediately out to sea again passing directly thro the blockading fleet, who were so busy celebrating their victory that they did not notice the passing of the ship which made a safe passage back to Nassau.

The pilots and their families throve wonderfully during this period of the war as the risk was great, also the pay and gold money which had not been seen in a long time began to make its appearance greatly to the joy of all beholders; and if the pilots had known so much about finance as they did about navigation they would most of them have been rich men today. But as usual everywhere when a man is known to have money, everybody wishes to share it by fair means or by foul, no matter which. But in accordance with the generous nature which mariners are apt to possess the money slipped from their possession very fast. They lent it to anybody they considered a friend without security and they spent very freely for everything they wanted and a great many things they did not want. If they had known that the time

32

would come when they would be pilots no longer, they
been desirous of saving their small fortunes for such an en.

CHAPTER TEN

The epidemic of yellow fever which made such ravages among the population was over, and there was great hope that it would not appear the next year, but still, they could not feel entirely easy in their minds on the subject. Germs might be hidden away in some unlooked for place awaiting development, but the people resolved to meet the future with all the equinimity [sic] they could command.

Capt. John W. Galloway had been relieved from command of the Coast Guard, and ordered to report for duty on a blockade runner. When he was next heard from it was to the effect that he had died of yellow fever at Nassau; and this was the second death from that disease among the pilots. Capt. Galloway was a man of great ability as a pilot, and much confidence was placed in him to meet any emergency. He was a sincere friend and those who knew him were filled with regret that he had gone from them to be seen no more.

Blockade running had now been carried on to such an extent that it seemed almost as if there were regular lines of steamships running to foreign ports. Their services to the Confederacy were great, as they brought food and clothing for thousands who were in the field fighting for their country, while their families were left at home to fare as they could without their natural protectors. It was with pleasure and pride that their fellow citizens looked upon the efforts which helpless women with cheerful faces were making to support their families. But it was sad to often meet women and children in the streets, wan, pale and dispirited and poorly clad. When they were sick, medical attendance was freely given them without reward or hope of reward. Many of them needed medicine, and food alone could bring color to their faded cheeks. But the women of the Confederacy were noble women even in poverty, and they made little or no complaint as long as they believed the war was waged for their good; and they waited patiently for the result. But the aspect presented by the town of Smithville was sorrowful indeed. The garrison with its beautiful grounds, and its shady walks where so many had taken pleasure in former days, was reduced to a ruinous condition. One day an officer, purporting to be an engineer, made his appearance and ordered that the beautiful row of cedar trees should be cut down, and that a battery of heavy guns should be erected for some purpose. It was not usual to place batteries of eight inch guns in the middle of a populous town where there were no soldiers to man these guns and no enemy in sight or expected. In order to get the required material to build the traverses between the guns, the soil of the entire town to the depth of several inches was dug up and carted away to build this battery. Batteries were also erected on Dutchman Creek, on High Bluff opposite Deep Water Point, and also at Reaves' Point. None of these batteries were ever manned by Confederate soldiers. But war does many things that are inexplicable and perhaps the engineers knew their business. As they never fired a gun from these batteries during the war, it was left for a Federal officer to take away the guns and level down the ground again to its former plane. These defenses were the only things the civilians who were left in the town complained of during the whole course of the war, and this was because they could not see in their unfamiliarity of military engineering, what it was done for. The citizens of Smithville and those all along the coast as far as Little River, now turned their attention to the manufacture of salt. There were two works in the town of Smithville, and as the works were inexpensive they made salt to amuse themselves and drive away dull care and sorrow. They hoped of course to make a little money with which to supply themselves with the necessities of life, but when they had money by the bushel, (Confederate money) and there was nothing to sell, they gave it up as a bad job.

On a dark and dreary night during this period, Lieut. Cushing of the U.S. Navy with a small boat's crew slipped noiselessly from the blockade and landed in Smithville. The object of this expedition was to capture the Confederate General and his staff whose headquarters were in Smithville. As it happened the General had gone to Wilmington and was not at home to receive his unwelcome guests; but they captured two of his staff officers, marched them to the boat and went out of harbor unobserved with the captured officers; and also sentries were placed at short distances all along the beach. They were not seen or hailed and nothing was known of this raid until the next morning. On his return General Hubert was much astonished to find his officers absent from duty. This was one of several daring expeditions made by this Federal officer who was reported to have gone to Wilmington several times and walked about the town without being discovered. We shall see more of this daring officer later on.

As these things were going on a Confederate soldier came from Richmond in 1863 to Smithville on a visit to his relatives and brought the smallpox with him. The few citizens who remained in Smithville were terror-stricken and they felt that all the misfortunes which attend humanity in this life had now come to wipe them and their families off the face of the earth. There was no vaccine virus within the limits of the Confederacy that was known and they therefore felt themselves obliged to take their chances. The smallpox spread with fearful rapidity until every house in the town was full of it and it was the most virulent epidemic of that disease ever known and every case presented the appearance most repulsive. The odor pervaded every house and even the streets and there were only a small number of immunes to bury the dead. There were some cases of smallpox among immunes and one man who had had the disease and who had been badly marked had it very lightly. The blessing conferred upon humanity however by vaccination was perfectly well marked. Almost all who had been vaccinated in infancy or in early years were perfectly safe which they soon discovered greatly to their joy. I here take occasion to say that the doctors of 75 years ago were very particular to vaccinate every child so soon as possible after its birth, and I regret also to say that this practice has been very much neglected in late years mostly I think from carelessness and neglect on the part of the parents.

Now having related some of the sorrows which befell Smithville, it can be said that the people who were left breathed more freely, for "hope springs eternal in the human breast," and they hoped with some

Figure 2. The U.S. Quarantine Office, left, on the Southport Waterfront. The Frink home is seen in the center. The Stuart House, on the right, was a famous landmark inn operated by Kate Stuart.   Photo copied with permission from *The State Port Pilot.*

degree of assurance that they were safe. The Confederate authorities medical or otherwise, had found out by sad experience that war was not the only thing that required attention, and having discovered that by allowing the military authorities to drive a health officer from the decks of a ship filled with the yellow fever they had done a bad thing for the Confederacy. They therefore appointed Dr. John Meares of Wilmington as inspector and quarantine physician, and directed him to go to Smithville, and take up his abode there; to inspect every ship that came in thro the blockade, and if found infected to detain her as long as he might think necessary. Dr. Meares was eminent as a physician, but inexperienced in the manner of treating yellow fever. He performed his duty however, faithfully and to the best of his ability, but he was not provided with the means of isolating vessels from the public. Then in the early part of 1864 a blockade running steamer came into port, having on board pilot Anderson of Smithville, who had the yellow fever and perhaps others. Pilot Anderson was in the last extremity of yellow fever as the ship approached the blockade; and it was necessary to get through the blockade or lose his ship. On being apprised of the danger, he told the captain to have him carried to the deck on his cot, and he would direct the helmsman how to steer. The ship arrived in port in safety, but was fired upon while this pilot was sick onto death and directing the helmsman. The ship anchored opposite Deep Water Point, where this brave pilot died in a few hours in sight of his native land, as his mother stood at the open door ready to receive him. This was the third pilot who died while performing his duty. There being no guard boat placed around or near the ship, persons went on board from Smithville and contracted the disease of which they died in a few days; but not before they had communicated the disease in the town to those who died also.

CHAPTER ELEVEN

To speak of the inhabitants of Smithville at this stage of affairs is almost a contradiction of the truth. They consisted of but few old men incapable of military service, a few pilots who were awaiting orders to go on board a ship ready to sail, the wives and children of soldiers who were away in Virginia in the army and the families of pilots who had gone away and had not returned. It was reported that many of the pilots had been captured and were now in northern prisons from Boston to Baltimore awaiting exchange or such other fate as might befall them. There was also in Smithville one company of Confederate soldiers and the headquarters of the Commissary and Quartermaster's department. These were in charge of Major John Blount and his two clerks. Mr. and Mrs. Fred Robinson, Mr. John E. Lippit and his wife also occupied quarters in Smithville. There were also two ladies from Washington, N.C., visitors of Major Blount. The Rev. Mr. Greer was also in Smithville and held services in St. Phillips church. Mr. Prioleau and his son and two daughters, Dr. Frink, his wife and daughters had returned here from the interior of the state which they found was no safer than Smithville. Miss Mary Catherine Lord was also here visiting at the Frinks. She afterwards married the late Rt. Rev. A. A. Watson. Mr. Sidney Lanier and his brother, the former of whom was afterwards highly distinguished at the north as well [as] at the south as the foremost poet in America. He was a most skillful performer upon the flute and it was related of him that he played himself out of various prisons by his musical skill which was really wonderful. A feeble effort was therefore made among these people to have a little social pleasure which none of them had had for some years. It was somewhat after the manner of Nero playing among the flames of burning Rome.

Mr. Owen D. Holmes, and family and Dr. John H. Hill were on their plantations of Kendal and Lilliput trying rather vainly to keep up their spirits as there were newspaper reports that Fort Fisher would shortly be attacked by a great force of the enemy. The writer well remembers (and at this period of time it seems like a huge joke) that Doctor Hill insisted that if the Yankees came about his plantation that

Figure 3. The Brunswick Inn on Bay Street where it meets Atlantic Street, left, was owned by Dr. Curtis. The house in the middle was known as the old Morse home. Notice the widow's walk on the roof. Dr. Frink owned the house at the far right. The Brunswick Inn, destroyed by hurricane Hazel in October 1954, stood across the street from these houses.   Photo copied with permission from *The State Port Pilot.*

he would have one shot at them at any rate; but he thought better of this the next day when he gathered together his negroes and started to the interior of the country. Mr. Owen Holmes did the same thing and escaping as they thought into Samson county where they thought no enemy would ever discover them. But sad and bitter was their experience for they got right in the tract of Sherman and his bummers and all the negroes who had been so carefully taken to this place of safety went over to the enemy and assisted them in their work of destruction and depredation.

The gentlemen and ladies heretofore mentioned, who tried to forget the war and have a little amusement here in Smithville, actually accomplished their purpose to a considerable extent. Most of them met together in the evenings, and beguiled the time with delightful music; and while the cannon at Fort Fisher and Fort Caswell were being inspected and put in condition for a battle this little company in Smithville were singing "Dreams," "What are The Wild Waves Saying," and so delightfully they passed the time that it really seemed as though peace had actually come. But only a few days after these happy times a great fleet of ships of war and their attendant transports under command of General B. F. Butler, sailed down the coast and dropped their anchors in front of Fort Fisher. These ships presented a magnificent spectacle to lookers on in Smithville who were at safe distance from the battle. They opened fire shortly after noon in Dec. 1864, and the most terrific bombardment of modern time ensued. The writer was informed by Gen. Whiting, who was in command of the district, and Col. Lamb who commanded the fort, that sixty thousand shells were fired into the fort on that afternoon. As night approached it seemed to the spectators in Smithville, that the fort must certainly be in the hands of the enemy. There was a very small force in the Garrison at Fort Fisher, and they were not veterans either. They consisted mostly of the last levy upon the Confederacy, and were mostly boys not inured to danger or the hardships of battle; and there were very few troops in the vicinity, by which the fort could be re-inforced. It was therefore a great surprise to the people to hear the next morning that the fort had not been captured, but that Gen. Butler had sailed away with his great fleet and given up the contest. It was reported however in a few days, that the Government had removed General Butler from his command, and that a General of great ability had been chosen to command the fleet, and that the attack would shortly be renewed. So the condition of affairs in Smithville assumed a peaceful aspect again. By this time there were very few left in Smithville of either soldiers or citizens, and all who could get away from the place withdrew to a safer locality. The Q.M. and Commissary stores were removed partially and Maj. Blount and his family and their visitors left Smithville. Then there was another period of waiting. In about three weeks the great fleet returned, and the attack re-commenced under the command of Admiral Porter. A large force was landed upon the beach above the fort, and they stretched across the narrow neck of land from the ocean to the Cape Fear river. Nothing could be seen of the enemies' ships or what they were doing, at Smithville; but the bombardment was incessant and after twenty four hours the fort was captured by assault about 9 o'clock P.M. January 15th., 1865. The first intimation they had in Smithville of the result, was when the bombardment ceased, and there [w]as seen to be a great display of fireworks of every description which announced the fact that the fort had fallen. All was now quiet in Smithville and it remained so until the next night when it was seen that Fort Caswell and all the forts in the vicinity were on fire. As the flames spread from fort to fort the most terrific explosions occurred, shaking the very earth, and announcing the fact that all the forts below Fort Fisher and at the mouth of the river had been abandoned and the troops withdrawn. The troops manning these forts marched down the beach to a crossing about four or five miles below and crossed by the mainland, continuing their march in the direction of Wilmington. The few soldiers who were left in Smithville followed this army, and left Smithville a silent and deserted place, whose inhabitants wondered what was to happen next. But the next day after the capture of Fisher, heavy cannonading was heard on the eastern side of the river, and it was evident that the enemy were trying to make their way up that side to capture Wilmington. But the country on that side of the river was not suitable for an advance, and firing ceased, and it soon became evident that an attack upon Wilmington on that side of the river had been abandoned and that they would cross the river and renew the attack on the western side. They had secured a number of negroes to show them the way, and transports carrying thousands of soldiers with their baggage and stores landed in Smithville, and marched through the town. They marched to the rear of the place to the number of about five thousand men and encamped for the night. The citizen population of Smithville which were few in number, now had an opportunity to see something of war; and it seemed to them that the enemy were as numerous as the sands upon the seashore. The next morning they resumed their march up the river guided by Lem Brown, a negro, besides other negroes. Fort Anderson and all the other forts on the west side of the river were evacuated and there was little fighting on their way to Wilmington which fell into their hands without a shot being fired.

Now Smithville had relapsed again into its state of quiet, but not the quiet of former days, for there were "camp followers" and "bummers" in the rear to pick up anything which might come to hand, which amounted to very little. Negroes however reaped a rich harvest in the shape of clothing from soldiers and blankets of which the forest was strewn.

On reviewing the situation it seemed as though Smithville must be the most lonely, deserted spot upon the face of the Southern Confederacy. But there were a considerable number of wounded men belonging to both armies who were left in buildings in the town which had been occupied by the Confederacy. One or two doctors remained to care for the wounded men.

CHAPTER TWELVE

Although civil government had practically ceased to operate, for a long time a few of the old officials called a meeting of the citizens to consult as to what should be done.

It had been observed that two of the enemies' ships had come around Frying Pan Shoals and were anchored off Fort Caswell. It was concluded that they had arrived to take possession of those abandoned fortifications. This proved to be true for soon men were seen on the parapets of Fort Caswell engaged in erecting a flag staff from which the Stars and Stripes could float upon the breeze. The citizens of Smithville therefore determined to raise a white flag on the flag staff which stood in the Garrison and to send a boat containing a committee of prominent citizens bearing also the white flag, to meet the enemies' boat which was seen coming around the point. Appointing one of the committee spokesman they rowed out boldly into the middle of the stream where they met a boat from the enemy flying the United States flag. Captain Cushing it appears, had turned up again and the surrender of the town of Smithville was made to him. In a few appropriate remarks Captain Cushing was informed that the town had been entirely evacuated by troops and that it's population consisted of women and children and a few non-competent men who requested that he would protect their rights as citizens. Both boats then turned towards Smithville and landed at the Garrison wharf from which place the committee departed to their homes; but before doing so they were informed by Capt. Cushing that the citizens must bring all fire arms in their possession and surrender them to those in charge of the boat. A few of his men were directed to proceed to the officer's quarters of Fort Johnston and take possession and to haul down the white flag upon the flag staff and to hoist the flag of the United States in it's place. This concluded the ceremony of the surrender. But there was more yet to be done. A large assembly of negro men, women and children had collected at the boat in order to greet their "saviors," and to fall upon their necks and kiss them if such liberty should be allowed. Captain Cushing then addressed the sable crowd and informed them that they were free, that they were in all respects equal to the whites and would be so treated. In order to make sure that this was true he directed that they (the negroes) should form a procession and give three cheers which they did saying, "God bless Massa Lincum we'se free" and "Massa Lincum is comin in a day or two to bring each of us a mule and a deed for forty acres of land." The procession then started to move, amid wild cheering for "Massa Lincum." There were some small United States flags scattered amongst the crowds which they waved frantically in the air crying, "hallelugah, hallelugah." The procession then moved through the garrison to Moore St. a motley crowd dressed in every conceivable style bearing banners of anything that was a bright color and they started down Moore St. amid cheering for "Massa Lincum." They marched down Moore St., to Boundary St., up Boundary to Nash St., up Nash to the Garrison where they dispersed. Thus ended the surrender of Smithville which was now in military possession of the United States. The officers of the United States Naval ship "Monticello" under command of Capt. Cushing took possession of the Garrison building where they established themselves as comfortably as they could. Re-inforcements arrived from the ships and sentinels were placed all around the town with orders not to allow any one to pass out or in without written permission.

In the procession which had marched around the town was "Uncle Gibb," and his posterity. "Uncle Gibb" had been treated during his entire life as kindly as any white citizen in the town. He had a house to live in, plenty of food and clothes, and a horse and dray; and it was difficult to perceive how he had bettered his condition by freedom; but he soon found out as he was brought a prisoner into the Garrison for some alleged offense. Here he was tied up by the thumbs to an oak tree which stood there, and hoisted till his toes barely touched the ground. This was done in full view of his own sister who was cook in an adjoining kitchen, and who fainted and fell at the awful sight. He thus had an opportunity to find out whether the new friends of the colored race were any better then the old friends who had treated him with such kindness.

The ceremony attending the surrender having been completed, the boat containing the plunder was dispatched back to the "Monticello," and there being apparently nothing to do on shore, the sailors were given liberty and the officers proceeded to enjoy themselves. The sailors spread themselves over the town, and proceeded first to inspect the public buildings. They broke open the court house and it's offices, tore up such papers as they found lying around among which happened to be the entire record of the Court of Equity and scattered them about the streets. They went to the Academy building in which was a Masonic Hall, and stole the jewels of the Order, and carried them on board the ship. It is fair however to say that these jewels fell into the hands of the ship's surgeon who being a Mason himself, returned them as soon as possible to the lodge. They did not however disturb any of the churches of which there were but one or two, one Episcopalian and one Methodist. The Episcopal church had been thoroughly desecrated by others before the town surrendered. This state of things continued for a few days only, when this force of sailors were relieved of duty, and the 149th New York Regiment was sent to occupy the position. This regiment was composed of good and well-disciplined men under command of Col. A. M. Barney, who proceeded to restore order at once in the town, the soldiers commanded by him being well disciplined.

In this way friendly relations were established between the military and the civilians, who now considered themselves safe. During the period of three or four months in which he commanded Fort Johnston, there was order throughout the town, and nobody was permitted to be disturbed.

Transports were placed upon the river, running every day to Wilmington, and these cities were once again in friendly relations to each other; but there was great confusion in Wilmington for a long time. Wilmington was a centre to which all sick and maimed, and disabled soldiers were brought to embark on steamships which carried them away to their Northern homes and hospitals. It was a pitiable sight while they were waiting for transportation, to see hundreds of them sitting around on doorsteps or any place where they could find rest. The Quartermaster and Commissary Departments which were on duty in Wilmington, assisted these disabled men as fast as they could; but the war was not yet over, and the military government had to be established in Wilmington. It was not long before the end came. The Confederate soldiers who had evacuated all the places in the vicinity of Wilmington, marched up by way of the railroad, and concentrated there under the command of General Jos. E. Johnson, and the battle of Bentonville was fought, in which Col. Robt. G. Rankin was killed,

44

and Col. John D. Taylor so severely wounded as to lose one of his arms.

I shall not pursue the subject of the war any further, it being evident that it was approaching its end, and I am not trying to describe anything minutely that does not effect the destinies of Smithville.

After the surrender of Gen. Lee at Appomattox, there was not much more to relate of military proceedings. The Confederate army disintegrated, and the soldiers who remained hastened to their homes as rapidly as they could. Both Smithville and Wilmington remained in military occupation of the Federals.

The description of the landing of General Cushing's boat, and of his famous order to the people of Smithville, to wit: That they should bring all firearms and weapons of offence, and dangerous to human life was obeyed to the minutest particular. Since the citizens remaining in Smithville consisted almost entirely of women, children and pilots it is natural to suppose that the weapons they surrendered were extremely varied in their character, and we may also reasonably suppose that there were old Queen's arms of the Revolutionary period, bird guns and shot guns of all kinds including pistols of the flint lock variety, probably without flints; that there were bludgeons, swords, guns and steel traps. Also since it had been some years since the blessed period which we now call Christmas, which was so wonderful and important to the world by the arrival of the Prince of Peace, that the children of Smithville must have turned up all their little weapons including blow-guns, spring guns, and every other variety of gun which so delights the childish fancy, and which had been for four years laid aside and almost forgotten; and the pilots brought those weapons which appertain to their calling somewhat, viz: harpoons and fish hooks; and that all these things were deposited in the boat in pursuance to military order number 1; and that all these weapons had been transported to the great ship lying outside the harbor, in strict obedience to orders. Now it is a most interesting question what has become of all the weapons which it was necessary to capture in order that the slaves might peacefully and without danger traverse the streets of the town, and celebrate the great event which to them seemed only second to that other arrival which we have mentioned as the arrival of the wonderful, the Councellor the Great, and Almighty Lord. Now they could wave their flags, and shout "bress de Lord," and "Massa Lincum for what he has done for us," without fear of old Marsters or Misses, or any other dangerous person whatever. We hope that this collection of weapons may sometime come to light in the great museum which will illustrate the capture of Smithville and "de close ob de wah."

CHAPTER THIRTEEN

It would take much time and space to describe everything that happened for the next two years. The Confederates who belonged in Brunswick county and Smithville were working their weary way homeward. The pilots who had been in prison were released and came slowly home.

Smithville had seen continual change; white troops and colored troops went and came according to orders. Some of them were mustered out in the Garrison here and proceeded immediately to Washington. As a general thing the troops had been quiet and under control of their officers. The Freedman's Bureau had established itself in Smithville and was constantly issuing rations to negroes who applied for them. There was a detachment of Yankee "school marms" who sat down here, and instructed the young colored "idea how to shoot." The army stragglers and carpet baggers and bummers and "school marms" continued the work of instructing the colored voter. Many important ideas had to be instilled into the vacant minds of the colored man who was to be a voter, a legislator, a judge, a member of Congress and makers of laws to govern the white race who were mostly disqualified from exercising any function. What the colored man had to learn was important. He had to learn that he was free and the equal of the white man; he had to learn that he must not take off his hat while speaking to a white man or woman and that above all things they must not address them as master or mistress, and to continually remember "dat de "publikin party" had freed him from slavery and that if he had voted for a Democrat for any office he would immediately be put back into slavery. These principles were necessary as preliminaries to an election. Should he be ordered he was to march to the polls to the music of the drum and under colors of the United States. As he could not read his vote he was ordered to supply himself with tickets from certain persons designated for that purpose. All these things and many more had to be taught to the negro because in the beginning his mind was blank but he was apt to learn these foundation principles upon which his freedom was guaranteed. But these things which have been described only applied to Smithville. It was intended by the rulers of the Republican party at Washington under the lead of Thaddeus Stevens, Charles Sumner, Wendell Philips and a host of others scattered through the northern country, and by the Congress of the United States so far as they could govern it, that reconstruction should begin with the confiscation of all lands heretofore owned by the whites and cultivated by slaves. That the white owners should be made to surrender their rights in favor of the ex-slaves. It was expected that by this means the land owners should be made paupers and the negroes rule the country. President Lincoln whose policy was beneficial and intended to heal all the injuries which the war had inflicted had been assassinated by the bullet of John Wilkes Booth. The ultra members of the Republican ring made a great pretense of mourning but in reality they believed that an obstruction to their fiendish policy had been removed. Vice president Johnson had become president and it was his policy to carry on the beneficent ideas of Mr. Lincoln, but that did not suit the view of Thaddeus Stevens and his band of conspirators, so they brought articles of impeachment against President Johnson and would have succeeded in removing him had it not been for a very few voters which they could not control. Failing in reconstructing the country on this plan they passed laws which rendered President Johnson powerless to do anything and vested the powers which should have been exercised by the president, in Congress.

They repudiated what President Johnson had done in the way of reconstruction and put the South under military government. The first election in North Carolina was held by orders issued through General Canby commanding the department in which North Carolina was situated. This election was held under rules and regulations of military orders emanating from headquarters from Charleston. A ticket was formulated which consisted of such men as the ultra Republicans approved. The Democrats held an election and nominated a ticket. The ballot boxes were sent to General Canby for the votes to be counted and certificates of election were issued to such as could be trusted.

Hence originated the first Legislature which was held after peace had been declared. What they did is a matter of history. Brunswick county was represented in this Legislature by a carpet bagger named Edwin Legg an ex-suttler of the Federal army. It is not proposed to go into any description or criticism of the Legislature, for it was a body of men to forget rather than remember. The election held in Smithville was the first trial which the new voters went through, and was intended to establish their capacity to be voters and their strength in this district. All Federal offices had been filled by Republicans, who exercised all their powers to insure a solid negro vote. The negroes were gathered together and provided with votes and marched to the polls where their votes were inspected to insure that they had not been tampered with. The military were stationed within convenient call in case any obstruction was offered to prevent the voter from voting the "publican ticket." The interest with which every negro voted was a terror because he was instructed that a continuance of his freedom depended upon his voting against his former master; and he has never forgotten the lesson then instilled in his mind. But it is beyond the purpose of this paper to go into descriptions of the outrageous work which was carried on during this time. It continued until the great statesman and patriot, Zebulon B. Vance redeemed the state from negro domination. After his election the people breathed more freely, and felt that they were once more to direct public affairs. Even Brunswick county which held a large negro majority, once more passed into the control of conservative men. Through all this trying period there were a few men scattered through the county who

48

labored zealously to bring about relief, and finally better councils prevailed so that the white population controlled the county and every part of it. I will merely in concluding this chapter say; that had Abraham Lincoln been permitted to live he would have carried out a humane policy which would have brought relief from the dreadful calamity which the war had entailed and the whole people of the United States would have been happy and prosperous, and the miseries which have come upon us would have been entirely averted. Many years ago we might have had the same result in which we now enjoy peace and prosperity.

Our universities and our public school system had been re-established upon a sure basis, and our young men are going out to establish the reputation of our state in every branch of commerce, and every branch of scientific culture and improvement. There is now no real reason why the citizens of the United States should be divided by ultra partizan ideas. We have had a long and tempestuous journey through rough seas of political strife but our common country has been elevated to a higher plane of unselfishness which will now become a part of the world's history, and when that history is written it is to be hoped that what we have gone through will be the mere episode in the history of the United States which will not disturb the mental quiet and peacefulness in which we ought to remain as friends and companions as brothers in arms on land and sea with our flag floating in every harbor of the world as the token of our greatness as a united people.

In reviewing the period which elapsed from the close of the war up to the election of Governor Vance it will be seen that wise and patriotic men whose names should be known and inscribed upon the pages of history were laboring continually to restore peace and prosperity and in doing this they had to act with great judgement and discretion. It is impossible to name all these men, but it may be said with truth that they were all Democrats. This writer dies not remember the name of one white Republican who, during this period acted upon any other principle than to retain power in the hands of his party. While the Democrats of Brunswick county, and I think of the whole state, acted on the principle of restoring peace and making a genuine, happy and reunited country in whose breast patriotism was the moving principle. Col. John D. Taylor, William Watters, Owen D. Holmes, D. S. Cowan, Saml. R. Chinnis, D. C. Allen, John M. Bennett, John Mercer, Wilson McKethan, Saml. and Jabez Frink, John H. Mintz, D. L. Butler, Jesse Lancaster, Peter Rourk, Rufus Galloway, David Gilbert, S. J. Standland, Thomas G. Drew, Francis Moore, W. G. Curtis, and a host of others equally as good, whose names there is not sufficient space to record, were the men who worked in season and out of season to bring back peace to Brunswick county and to the state. These men were assisted as opportunity offered, by nearly every member of the legal profession who practiced at the Brunswick bar, and they were always ready to come over from New Hanover and other counties to help us. The names of those who acted on the other side are well known to this community, but I will not record the names of one of them. They went by the names of "black republicans," "fushionists," and generally speaking their principles were anything to beat the Democrats, and they remain without the love of the citizens of Brunswick who belong to the Democratic party.

CHAPTER FOURTEEN

We shall now lay aside for a brief period the subject of war and reconstruction but we must say here that the war had developed and shown the great resources of both north and south. The north had shown by the war that it possessed almost unlimited power. Great as was the war it had not exhausted the north which had had the world's power ready to come to it's assistance whenever disaster had befallen its arms. It was but a reasonable conclusion therefore, that the south must give up the contest. Had it not been for the institution of slavery, the south could not have maintained itself as long as it did, for the south had put all its men of fighting age into the conflict. Old men, young men and boys had joined the army of the Confederacy, and it had fought with brilliant energy and enthusiasm. Their leaders had been of greater military capacity than those from the north, and their brilliant strategy had excited the admiration of the whole world. In particular the great genius of General Robert E. Lee which was displayed in all the battles between the Union and the Confederacy. In all arms of the service they had been almost invincible and they were only weak in point of number. But it must be set down to the credit of the slaves of the south, that although in their untutored minds the desire of freedom existed, yet it did not display itself in fighting to gain that freedom. They remained at home on their plantations and worked diligently for the "old marster" who had gone to the war and for the "old mistisses and young mistisses" who remained at home and who with unflagging zeal did what they could to assist in the great work which laid before the soldiers in the field. The majority of the slaves remained faithful to the last, and made the corn, potatoes, cotton and all the agricultural products which were produced on southern soil. Thus the slaves made it possible for the armies of the Confederacy to exist because men will not fight when they know that their wives, and children are starving. A few of them comparatively speaking, were mustered into the service of the Union, mostly on the frontier while a few of them all along the coast escaped to the blockading ships. But the intellect of the negro was not sufficient to originate liberty nor did they know what to do with it after they got it; therefore they fell into the hands of designing men, politicians, carpet baggers, scallawags and school "marms" who emigrated to the south in great numbers all assisting to make true their contention that the negro was equal to the white man.

In the process of reconstruction it was the chief aim of the politicians to make the negroes fit for the liberty which had come to them without their efforts. Since they were to be free, wise councils on the part of the Democratic statesmen of the north would have enabled Mr. Lincoln and others of his class to reconstruct the Federal Union without the terrible scenes which were enacted by Republican politicians and all the southern states would have gone back peacefully into the Union without the difficulties which continually arose and made the process of reconstruction by the Republicans almost an impossible task. But instead of this, the time consumed in reconstruction occupied many years of the wildest confusion which has been heretofore described in these papers and now time with leaden wings had passed away, had traversed the space consumed by war, pestilence and famine and reconstruction, and peace seemed to be hovering over the land.

All the business operations which had been discontinued, resumed life again and work began everywhere where the white man was in possession of the field. Plantations were again put in order, and the splendid rice plantations which bordered the Cape Fear river began to look green and promised fruitful crops. The waters of the Cape Fear and the Atlantic gleamed with their white sails. The merchants of Wilmington and producers of all commercial crops began the various operations connected with their businesses. The laborers who had returned home carrying their axes and turpentine hackers with them, now resumed their tools and returned to the forests. The distillers in Wilmington prepared for business. The Government of the United States showed itself willing to assist in such great works as the improvement of rivers and harbors. Men of energy and enthusiasm had been sent to Washington and appropriations were procured for carrying on work on the river and bar. General William P. Craighill, an engineer of distinction was appointed to take charge of the works on the Cape Fear river with his able assistant, Mr. Henry Bacon and the work was taken up where it had been left at the beginning of the war. It was determined then to close up the new inlet and turn all the waters into one channel. This was a great work but not too great for money, skill and energy to accomplish and it was accomplished after several years of persistent labor and results immediately followed, showing the gradual deepening of the river and bar. This was eminently satisfactory not only to the merchants of Wilmington but to all citizens of North Carolina who were interested in commercial pursuits. The results were not precisely as expected but they showed a deep harbor and plenty of water on the bar. It showed also that a good channel up the river could now be dredged out which would remain more or less permanent. If shoals accumulated up the river they could be easily removed by the expenditure of money. It was at this crisis of affairs that certain merchants in the city of Wilmington of whom Mr. R.E. Heide was the pioneer, determined to establish direct shipments to the various ports of Europe which had hitherto been sent by New York and northern cities. It was necessary to accomplish this, that square rigged vessels such as barques and brigs should be used and the successful results of several voyages established this foreign commerce permanently for the city of Wilmington. The business of making turpentine and distilling it into spirits and rosin was resumed with great activity and continued for several years. As a natural consequence of this great business the turpentine was exhausted and the business began to decline. The great pine regions of South Carolina, Georgia and Florida were brought into use and the centre of this trade had to be transferred to Savannah, Ga. Of course no human foresight or energy could prevent this, as the pine forest must of necessity yield up this vital fluid, and go into a state of exhaustion in a certain length of time. This condition was shown conclusively by a gradual but sure decrease in the number of sailing ships which came to the port of Wilmington for cargoes. If Wilmington had not possessed men of great commercial ability, and untiring energy, the commerce of Wilmington would have entirely ceased. Cotton must be substitute, and the soil and climate of the south was such that this business had only to be started to insure permanent success and this was done by the firm of Alexander Sprunt & Sons, merchants of Wilmington.

The most important results of the opening of the Cape Fear river were the facts plain to all observers that North Carolina now had a deep water port all the way from the new inlet which had been closed, to the ocean; and this port was to be permanent and not liable to be filled up or even obstructed by shoals. It was also plainly seen that no more great appropriations would be necessary because the swift and strong current of the Cape Fear would sweep everything of an obstructing nature through its length into the ocean. It seemed to the people that this new harbor deserved a new name, and it was therefore changed from Smithville to Southport. This was the first time in the history of the world that North Carolina possessed a deep water

Figure 4. The Curtis home, left, on Moore Street in Southport.
Photo copied with permission from *The State Port Pilot*.

harbor. It was natural to suppose that North Carolina would immediately utilize the advantages she possessed, by building up a town of considerable importance at the mouth of the river. But the building of a new city, and new lines of commerce is a slow business, and it requires men of large capital who are able to see far in the future to develop a new city. Up to 1905 no new city had been developed and the most that can be said of it is that at this time the attention of the world has been directed to it with a considerable probability that somebody will do something before much more time rolls by.

CHAPTER FIFTEEN

Smithville, which about fifteen years ago became Southport, was at the time when these reminiscences began in 1848, a small town at the mouth of the Cape Fear river, commercially of no importance whatever. It became however through the investigations of enterprising people of the city of Wilmington, a place of refuge during the summer months from mosquitoes and malaria. The site on which this small town was built had been given by Governor Benjamin Smith for the purpose of laying out a town with streets and public square, and other privileges pertaining to an incorporated town. The General Assembly of North Carolina incorporated this town under the name of Smithville, and it was surveyed and laid out by a competent engineer into streets, squares and city lots. A few of these lots were sold at first, and persons of no small importance purchased them and built houses upon them, moved their families to Smithville and found it a place where they could enjoy life, it being free from all annoyances.

The streets were named after distinguished men who had gained their public distinction by acts which made them known throughout the state. Such names as Moore street, named for Judge Alfred Moore; Nash street, for General Nash; Howe street, for General Howe; Rhett street, for Colonel Rhett of South Carolina; Potts street and others, and a public square named Franklin square after Benjamin Franklin, which was devoted to public and charitable purposes.

The site upon which the town was laid out was of considerable military importance as was amply testified by the construction of a block house in the centre of the town, commanding the entrance to the river; and this fort was named Fort Johnston after a Governor of that name. Fort Johnston was built for defense against Indians mostly or perhaps for defense against artillery, the cannon of which at that date were of small size compared to those of the present day. There were embrasures for cannon and small arms, and wells dug inside showing that the block house or Fort Johnston was intended to stand a siege if there should be war at any time. The blockhouse was built before the fort, by the English government to protect the citizens from the Indians. This blockhouse after standing for one hundred and fifty years, was finally demolished by railroad promoters who moved to Smithville for the purpose of building a railroad. The old citizens looked on with disgust at the vandalism which was willing to destroy these monuments of colonial times for the purpose of merely putting a few more dollars in their pockets and causing the place to assume a more modern appearance which they thought would attract the attention of capitalists. Then it was that the proposition was made to change the name to the town and a petition signed almost unanimously by the citizens of Smithville was introduced in the Legislature, and after much discussion and some fierce opposition the petition was granted. It will be seen therefore that the site on which Smithville was laid out, had a history which was both ancient, and honorable. It had not degenerated except that at the time the town of Smithville was chartered, it was used solely for peaceable purposes but afterwards was the scene of most stirring events.

About 1763 Great Britain attempted to tax the colonies by means of the Stamp Act which excited the people very greatly, and they determined that it should not be carried out within the limits of North Carolina; and when Great Britain attempted to enforce the Stamp Act by armed force, they were met by the citizens of the town of Brunswick who seized and destroyed the stamps, and also the vessels which brought them.

It has been chronicled in these papers how Smithville has been devastated again and again by war, pestilence and almost by famine. The citizens of Smithville assisted in every way to promote the building up of the city of Wilmington, as did the citizens of Wilmington who could never have arrived at the distinction of being the greatest navel store market in the world, had it not been for the assistance of the pilots who lived mostly in Smithville. In all the strenuous efforts which Wilmington has made to be a city of importance, Smithville and Wilmington have acted together in all matters whose object it was to develop a great commerce. But when that great work of stopping up the New Inlet by building a stone dam across it had been completed, it was found that a great basin into which the largest ships could enter, and find a safe port of anchorage, and the depth of water on the bar increased to 25 feet, thus making it possible to build a great city where was once Smithville. The great object obtained was met with incredulity instead of joy. There was not a single port in the state of North Carolina in which a great commerce could have been transacted. The citizens of Smithville saw it, and they labored in season, and out of season, to introduce to the world the new harbor, but they had only the mails by which they could distribute this important information. Using this means, they did in the course of a few years, bring the subject to the attention of the public in all other states excepting North Carolina. It was shown conclusively by maps and charts, by reliable information obtained from the pilots, that there was actually the depth of water stated and that the cost of carrying on commerce would here be reduced to a minimum. It was also shown that Southport was nearer to the cities of the great west by sixty or seventy miles than any other port on the Atlantic coast. It was also in a convenient position for the exportation or importation of goods of all kinds from the West Indies and South America, that molasses and salt which had been heretofore brought from the West Indies to Wilmington and been distributed from thence could be brought to Southport, and be distributed all over North Carolina and the west now more conveniently and cheaply than from any other place. It was also shown, that vessels coming to Southport from any point south would avoid the dangers of Hatteras, which was, and is a dread to all who navigate the ocean. It was also shown for the great exportation of coal, Southport was the best point to start from. A great correspondence was held with people both of the north and west, and large numbers of railroad promoters came to Smithville and made thorough investigations, and so reported to business men in places from whence they came.

It was thought by the citizens of Smithville that Wilmington would take up these matters, and enterprises with great energy and avidity but such has not been the case and Wilmington with her railroad system running north and south has been a solid bar against this work, which meant the building of railroads from the east to the west. Lately, however this vigilance which prevented every attempt to develop the new harbor and its proposed railroad connections with the west has been somewhat relaxed. The newspapers published in Wilmington and throughout the state, have discovered now what ought to have been discovered twenty years ago and have taken up the subject of developing this North Carolina port, with considerable interest.

CHAPTER SIXTEEN

There is a history of Smithville in its ancient day then known as Fort Johnston, ancient because there is no one living to describe accurately its monuments, and its residences. Even the village cemetery can tell but little. Its tombs and its tablets are decayed and fallen into utter ruin but it is learned that many of these tombs contained the bodies of persons who have lived and been respected and whose good works have outlived even their tomb stones. There is no one at present living who lived in the days of Governor Benjamin Smith or who can tell from personal knowledge who lived in or who built most of the houses which stood in Smithville in 1848. Yet they were built for persons to live in who were gentlemen of culture and refinement. They possessed a style peculiarly their own and this style indicated beyond doubt that they had been built by skillful mechanics and had been occupied by gentlemen of the older time. Altho the architecture of their houses was of the simplest kind, still in every house were evidences of an aesthetic taste. Especially their taste ran in the direction of mantle pieces and stair cases with carved balusters for altho the houses were of one story there were always finished rooms in the attic as was plainly evident by the dormer windows which existed in every house and at these modern times are almost always leaky did not leak from the time they were built till the houses were in ruins. A dining room of considerable dimensions and sideboard which had been imported from England, also chairs and tables of solid mahogany, of that celebrated maker Chipendale which cannot be duplicated at the present day. There was sometimes a piano in the parlor manufactured by Broadwood of London, inlaid in the most beautiful manner with brass ornaments. Ten years ago there were specimens of these pianos sitting around in out of the way places or in the back yard altho the musical part of the instrument was worthless. The cabinet work was of the finest construction and did not come to pieces even when exposed to wind and weather. The bricks which were used for the construction of foundations and chimneys were brought over from England and many lie buried in the soil at the present day as good as when they were new. Enough was left of these buildings so that persons who now live could testify that they were built by careful and skillful mechanics and many of our modern mechanics could learn lessons from an inspection of this old work and would see at once that the houses and all parts of them were built by workmen who did honest work and built not only for money but also for reputation.

In 1848 there were at least twenty of these houses in Smithville, now there is not one. The question is an interesting one. Who built these houses and who lived in them? The owner, and the artisan have long crumbled to dust and their names are forgotten. In the year 1848 there was one exception to this rule. A large and perhaps at that time a palatial residence which might have been called the Governor's palace stood at the corner of Bay and Potts streets. It was built by Gov. Smith for his residence [and] stood on the most beautiful spot that then existed or does now exist on the Cape Fear River. It remained intact but neglected and out of repair up to the year 1858, when Mr. Thomas D. Meares became the owner of the property and finding it too much out of repair, took the old house down and built a modern structure upon the ruins. The old house was entered from the front and as you entered and looked towards the back your eyes would have rested upon a spacious and highly ornamental stair case which led to the upper rooms. On the lower floor, there were drawing rooms, on one side the grand entrance hall and a large dining hall thirty or forty feet long on the other side.

This summer home of Gov. Smith's was his favorite resort as its situation was healthy and overlooked the beautiful bay and Atlantic ocean and the island across the bay on the south formed a lovely green spot for the eye to rest upon making an agreeable variety in the scenery which without it would have been a water view somewhat monotonous and glaring to look upon a hot summer day. We may believe and in fact we know that this mansion was a home where lavish generosity and hospitality prevailed. Many distinguished visitors from both the Carolinas were entertained in this delightful home. Gov. Smith was prominent in all political affairs not only in North and South Carolina but in the new Republic which was being formed and it was after the death of Gov. Smith found to be a suitable residence for another governor of North Carolina, Gov. E. B. Dudley who made his summer home in Smithville in 1838. Mr. Thomas D. Meares erected a fine residence upon the ruins of the old house and it has maintained its reputation ever since the untimely death of Mr. Meares and many distinguished men including three other governors of North Carolina have enjoyed visits to this residence and perhaps have found it as pleasant a place to visit as it was a hundred years before. The old house built by Gov. Smith on this spot and many others in the town of smaller dimensions were probably designed and built by Benjamin Blany a man esteemed by every one who resided in Smithville as a man of fine abilities, generous, charitable, fond of field sports and a personal friend of Gov. Smith. He lies buried in the old cemetery at Smithville but his tombstone which has fallen into much decay revives the fact that he was a man of high character in every respect. There is at present standing but one house which may be called ancient in Smithville and that is the house now known as St. Philips rectory, but this house altho built of materials which had stood the ravages of time for a century or more does not display any of the architectural merits which reveal themselves so plainly in the houses which had been built more than a century ago by Benjamin Blany.

CHAPTER SEVENTEEN

It is curious to observe, in how the development of cities and states the ideas commercial or otherwise which stand at the foundation of progress can always be traced to the active brains of a few individuals and this is especially the case in the development of the city of Wilmington.

The turpentine interest was a great business in itself in Brunswick county but it had a serious drawback in 1849. The principle makers of turpentine in Brunswick county came originally from Pitt, Edgecomb and Craven counties. They came and purchased or leased lands which were throughout the county very attractive to this class of our fellow citizens. At the date above mentioned the trees had not been tapped, and there was great competition to see who could get the most of this valuable timber; they set the example to the original citizens of the county and they too commenced the business. Dropping the plough, and the hoe and planting of all kinds of field crops they began tapping the trees for turpentine and to hire large numbers of negroes to do the work. At the same time they began to tap the trees, they began to buy provisions; corn, bacon and molasses all those things which constituted rations. They hired all the negroes they could giving their notes at pretty high prices for the years work and as was the custom of that time getting their friends, and neighbors to endorse their paper. Having advanced to this stage of the business they proceeded to look over their property with great complacency and to discount their profits. What was the horror therefore of a great number of these men as they passed through the beautiful pine forest to see large numbers of these splendid trees showing signs of some direful disease which spread in one season over a large part of Brunswick county. The trees died, in some places all of them, leaving hundreds of acres with nothing but dead trees upon them; in other places half the trees more or less died and it was seen that the prospect was very gloomy and that their great expectations of profit must be disappointed. This disease apparently was confined mostly to Brunswick county and large losses were sustained by these enterprising men instead of great gains. Then in addition to these responsibilities were the notes which had to be paid at maturity. Large expenses were incurred for supplies for the turpentine laborers and farms on their hands were neglected with growing crops upon them. This disease was new and very remarkable and there was nothing which could be done to stop it. Fortunately it did not extend much beyond this county and lasted but one year; it was caused by an insect pest which bored through the bark and deposited their eggs under the bark which prevented the growth of the tree. Many turpentine makers were ruined but the business as it appeared in the city of Wilmington did not show any effects as it was confined to such a limited area. But farming which is the foundation of prosperity in any country was temporarily destroyed and that business had to be done over again from the beginning; new lands to clear, and new fences to build and new implements to be purchased. So that on the whole, the turpentine interests in Brunswick county did not prove to be profitable. If all who owned turpentine lands had only worked them to such an extent as they could with their own force and had not neglected the farm crops which were essential, they would have made money invariably and their trees would have lasted a very long time before they were used up.

But the active minds of the business men of Wilmington saw much farther ahead than did the proprietors and laborers of the pine forest. So they began to investigate the condition of the Cape Fear River with the improvement of its navigation as an ultimate necessity. They proceeded in a manner which will be hereafter described to improve the conditions by which they could get this great product of the pine tree into the markets of the world; they went on however the same way for many years and it was not until after the war that Mr. R.E. Heide, Mr. Alexander Sprunt and a few others conceived the idea of exporting the naval stores which were made in Wilmington, directly to Europe. The feasibility of doing this was denied by many but the originators of this new idea proceeded to develop their plans. At first only a few foreign ships could be induced to come into the Cape Fear River where they knew the navigation was bad for square rigged vessels. The few that tried it first being vessels of light draft and coming as they did from the British North American Provinces of England, Norway, Denmark and Germany and also a good many small brigs from the West Indies all of which loaded for European ports, and making safe voyages, soon distributed the news all over foreign ports that they could find cargoes of naval stores in the port of Wilmington, North Carolina. So the foreign export business was established on a sure foundation, and continued successful.

The Cape Fear River and the port of Wilmington was soon crowded with foreign vessels, increasing in size and draft as the river and navigation was improved. The fore-and-aft schooner which had been used exclusively, had to withdraw from the business, and this continued until the product of the pine began to diminish rapidly, and had to be discontinued in a large measure. The scenes which have been described, of sailing vessels coming in and going out of the harbor of Smithville had begun to be a thing of the past and now came another period of the low tide of prosperity; but there were men equal to the emergency; men who could do things when required and do them well, no matter how difficult; men who dared to seize the stamps, when sent over to tax the colonists; men who stood shoulder to shoulder with the men of Massachusetts in resisting all oppression by the mother country, and who finally accomplished the purpose on which they started.

CHAPTER EIGHTEEN

The men thought their rights were invaded by the Federal Government and did not hesitate to go to war with a power many times greater than they were, and who fought for four long years with the fortitude and bravery which has seldom been witnessed in the world's history. Now peace had succeeded to war and to a period called "reconstruction" which was worse than any calamity which had preceded it, and it had left the commercial city of Wilmington without commerce, or anything on which to build a commerce. At this time it seemed to be necessary that men of character previously mentioned should come forward with the energy which they possessed to develop the arts of peace and commerce. Fortunately one commercial house in the city of Wilmington was equal to the emergency. Mr. James Sprunt of the house of Alexander Sprunt & Sons proposed that cotton should be made the basis of a new commerce. But it was impossible even to make a respectable beginning with only sailing ships which were loaded with cotton for different foreign ports but it became evident immediately that this was too slow to give any hope of successful competition with other ports. Then Mr. James Sprunt determined to proceed personally to Europe, and see what he could do in the establishment of steam lines to foreign ports. There were many difficulties to overcome. Wilmington was not known anywhere in the outside world as a cotton port and the old merchants, ship masters and owners looked upon Wilmington as a port, where there was too little water on the bar and difficult and unsafe navigation up the Cape Fear River to Wilmington. But Mr. Sprunt knew that the depth of water was increasing by means of the new works which were inaugurated by the general government for the purpose of increasing the depth of water. Mr. Sprunt succeeded in convincing ship owners and merchants that they might try a few of their smallest steamships with safety.

It was therefore a surprise and a great pleasure to see these iron tramps, which though small in size, looked very large to those who were well accustomed to sailing vessels. At this point fears were expressed that the pilots would antagonize this new trade by means of stream tramps, but this was an imaginary difficulty purely, for the pilots concerned themselves about nothing excepting the vessel which required their services, and it was a point of honor to carry these vessels through the obstructions, and safe to Wilmington.

So in this small way the cotton trade of Wilmington began, and Messrs. Alexander Sprunt & Son, were found to be the parties who could handle the business successfully. Gradually, and year by year larger vessels were substituted for the smaller ones which had made safe trips without accident and the trade grew rapidly until it was found that steamships drawing twenty feet of water, some of them carrying over twenty thousand bales of cotton could make their trips to and from Wilmington as safely as from any other port on the South Atlantic coast. In this manner commerce was re-established in the port of Wilmington, and it consisted very largely of the single article of cotton export, which remains to the present day, when over three hundred thousand bales are shipped yearly, with a prospect of an increasing trade.

But it must be evident to every observer that large cities cannot be built up solely on one article of commerce. The next most important article, which is a necessity is coal. But Wilmington could not monopolize the article of coal; she is too far up the river to handle it successfully. Therefore her merchants changed their opinions and agreed that coal should be carried to Southport, where there is deep water and easy access to and from the ocean but this trade has not yet been developed.

There are signs however that it will soon become a fact that ships of the largest capacity will come to Southport for their cargoes. In these papers which have been written, the distance, though a short one, has been traveled in spite of the greatest natural obstacles which are not yet entirely removed but which will be before the Cape Fear river, Wilmington and Southport become cities and a port of recognized importance. To the energetic, and well directed action of the business men of Wilmington, will be due the credit when their object is finally accomplished.

CHAPTER NINETEEN

About twenty years ago the discovery of this new harbor in North Carolina had been published in many papers at the North and West, and the opportunities for developing it had reached the ears of capitalists. Promoters began to pour into Smithville from all parts of the West, and even from England.

One corporation was formed called "The South Atlantic & North Western R. R. Co." The promoters of this scheme were men of considerable ability. David Risley and J. B. Bilheimer were the names of the principal promoters. Apparently these promoters had some money of their own which they were willing to spend. They put a force of engineers in the field and surveyed a line through from Southport to Bristol, Tenn. All went favorably and the different counties through which the line was to pass were enthusiastic about the great benefit which would accrue to the state of North Carolina. The corporation was organized with a board of directors and a president and it was reported that a Trust Company in New York had promised to float its bonds. Then a second corps of engineers started from Smithville to locate the line. They proceeded about forty miles. Throughout North Carolina from Smithville to Bristol, Tenn., it was pronounced by the people living anywhere near the line that it was a grand enterprise, which would open North Carolina to the commerce of the west. So far the "bulls" had had full charge of the scheme; but it was time that the "bears" should have their "innings," and they immediately prepared to depreciate the value of the scheme, and the "bears" were even found in the company itself.

Brunswick county had subscribed large sums, and it was perfectly evident that the people, were almost unanimously in favor of the enterprise. But the money centers had been infected with distrust.

The locating corps of engineers were called in and all active work ceased.

It is not the purpose of this writer to go into particular description of the promoting schemes which had been launched since 1883. Suffice it to say, that they might be numbered by the dozens and no matter how influential the promoters of all or any of them have been, those who did not want the road to be built, have proved to be the strongest.

At the present time there is a plan said to be in course of promotion by capitalists having untold wealth; owning railroads and steamship lines to the West Indies to South America and having large coast-wise interests, because they have positive information, that Southport has a harbor equal to their wants, and they propose therefore to utilize it. But of what prospective value this information may be, must be left for time to develop.

As all matters of this kind belong to the present, and can be in no way connected with the reminiscences of the past, I leave this subject merely saying that it is a great pity that money and enterprise sufficient for the purpose cannot be found in North Carolina, so that some of the great schemes proposed could be carried out; particularly that one which will bring coal to our doors at as cheap rates as it is supplied to citizens and manufacturers at the north and west. Wilmington needs cheap coal and Southport needs cheap coal. Without it manufacturers cannot thrive, and the high price which individuals have to pay is simply ruinous.

On looking over these series of papers, it is plainly to be seen, that the tide of prosperity has ebbed and flowed many times since the turpentine industry was at its flood. Natural causes have caused prosperity to decline, and the great energy of Wilmington merchants, has caused it again to rise to a considerable height; but what is required, is that industries should be varied and large enough to keep the golden tide of prosperity always at high water mark.

We suggest with great deference to the opinion of others, that an ample supply of coal lies at the foundation of all kinds of prosperity. The city of Wilmington must offer to the world favorable conditions for all kinds of manufacturing, it must offer to the world good and cheap markets for all the productions required for the use of manufacturers and the thousands of operatives which they must employ. It must have a first class railroad to Southport where people can purchase building sites and build houses for permanent occupation for both winter and summer. The climate is eminently suited to this. The rich lands which are suited for trucking and farming purposes must be connected with Southport and Wilmington by fast lines of railroad.

Then, as it seems to the writer of these articles, Wilmington and Southport will be one and the same city, having the same interest and it would be a cheerful day for the inhabitants of this section when all petty jealousies are wiped away.

CHAPTER TWENTY

The low country of the southern states consists of a strip of land about one hundred miles long extending along the coast from the Atlantic and Gulf coast for nearly their whole length. This immense territory is intersected by some large rivers and a great many small ones emptying into the Atlantic Ocean and Gulf of Mexico. There are many swamps of large size, and most of them are susceptible of being drained, and when drained they form the most fertile lands which this country can exhibit, producing immense quantities of corn; and so large has been this crop of corn in former years that these swamps were called the granary of the country.

The dweller in Smithville had previous to the closing up of the New Inlet, seen fleets consisting of hundreds of vessels loaded with corn coming through the New Inlet by which they saved a long voyage around Frying Pan Shoals on their way to Wilmington, Charleston, Savannah and all the Southern ports. These vessels were of fine construction. They were built in the sounds by the inhabitants themselves of that region. Probably as many more of the same size, loaded with the same cereal sailed along the northern coast, supplying the northern cities with corn.

It was a necessity of the turpentine business, because the farmers engaged in that business had abandoned their farms and made no corn and no pork and the laborers in the turpentine woods had to be fed with corn and meat which had to be purchased elsewhere. This was one of the misfortunes attending the turpentine business; that farming was neglected, the farm suffered to become dilapidated.

Turpentine being a cash business produced nothing but cash as the result of working the trees, and every farmer imagined he could see a golden harvest at the end of a year's work, but he did not see that he had nothing to do with making the price of his product which was fixed by speculators who engineered and controlled prices after the material had reached market, and made it impossible for the farmer and owner of the land to calculate with any certainty what would be the final result of his year's labor.

This great strip of land which was upon the sea coast and ran up the rivers, was covered with the most beautiful growth of pine trees that it was possible to imagine. Only here and there in the swamps and along the margins of streams, was there any other growth excepting pines and as the country was perfectly level and very little undergrowth to obstruct the vine it was often possible to see for miles a forest in which the giant boles of these pine trees ascended to the height of a hundred feet or more, and beneath, the ground was covered with grass and flowers. It was certainly a most beautiful prospect and one which could not be seen in any other country.

Not only were these forests beautiful, but they were valuable beyond any estimate which their owners were apt to make of them. The turpentine which might be made to flow from wounds in their surface made by the axe and turpentine hacker to bring large sums of money into the pockets of the owners and they were also more valuable than any other tree for building purposes.

In consequence of these values and others attached to a pine forest they were attacked with the vigor of desperation to get their products to market and no estimate was made of the loss which would accrue of the using up of these valuable trees. Hence it is now certain that the business was wasteful in almost every respect. If one now in the year 1905 goes out into these lands to examine them, he will find they have been hacked as high as the laborer can reach with a long pole and the turpentine exhausted in the tree never to be replaced; that their beauty is gone, and that here and there very frequently fire has gone through these inflammable trees and destroyed them outright and forever. That in consequence of burning the woods so that new grass could spring up every year for pasturage for cattle, the trees themselves have been burned and there is a desert exposed to view instead of the beautiful forest before described, and the visitor would be surprised to see that no trees of any kind have sprung up to make a second growth on the lands and he will be informed that this is because the woods are full of hogs who root up the ground and eat up every seed which accident or design may have deposited.

The farmer will deplore his improvidence, and wish he had not been so deeply infected with the mania which destroyed the county and value of his land to a great extent, and he will study how he can

69

recompense himself in some degree for what has been lost.

At this point the lumber getter makes his appearance, and proposes to buy every tree which will produce a railroad tie. He invades the swamps, and sees thousands of cypress trees, the growth of centuries perhaps, and he proposes to buy the trees or even lands upon which they grow. Here the owner sees his chance to make something, and so he sells the trees or rents or buys the land, and the work of getting railroad ties for northern market begins. Sawmills are established upon all the navigable streams, and soon the clang of the saws is heard in every place where there is a tree of what ever kind it may be; pines, cypresses, black gum and every other tree which can be shipped and manufactured into anything is cut and prepared for shipment.

The people of the state generally consent to this business and great corporations are chartered by the legislature.

Soon large schooners make their appearance for the purpose of taking on cargoes of railroad ties. The owners of these vessels and merchants, who may have become interested in this business, seek for every chance that may offer to reduce the cost of shipment and induce vessels to engage in the trade. They make it appear that the cost of pilotage is prohibitory to their business, therefore pilotage must be abolished, in which case the money paid to pilots would go into their own pockets. Thus the clearing of North Carolina of every useful trade goes on with fearful rapidity and the owners of the lands find themselves but very little richer on account of this business, and the glory and beauty of the scenery is destroyed forever.

CHAPTER TWENTY-ONE

It must not be considered, that because these papers have hitherto chronicled the rise and fall of Wilmington and also the rise and fall of Smithville along with it, that nothing had been done in Smithville of sufficient importance to be noted.

On the contrary many things have happened which has effected not only Smithville itself, but the State of North Carolina.

Neither history or tradition records that any attention of consequence was paid to education or public schools previous to 1815. There was a tradition of roving schoolmasters from the old country who traveled about teaching schools here and there as they could find enough pupils to give them support. These men would teach a short while in a place, then move on to some other field. Some of them were dilapidated gentlemen, who passed as graduates of Oxford or Cambridge, but none of them seemed to be of much value to the cause of education. But about the year 1850 Mr. Jeremiah Murphy moved to Smithville for the purpose of establishing a school. Mr. Murphy was a very agreeable gentleman, reliable and a man of fine character and abilities. He was a scholar and a gentleman of varied talents. He was well known to the writer as a genial companion

Figure 5. School building on Franklin Square. (Copied from *The State Port Pilot*)

and good friend. He, with other friends, took an active interest in the promoting of teaching, for which he was well fitted, being a teacher by profession, well versed in the classics, and in all branches of mathematical science and polite literature. Besides he had a very interesting family consisting of his wife and several children all of whom were calculated to exercise a refining influence upon the community.

Mr. Murphy saw at once the necessity of a good and permanent school at Smithville, and he, with others, immediately set about the promotion of a permanent one. But there was no school house in the town, and it was a matter of prime necessity to have a good school house, if there was to be a good school. The matter was at once discussed among the people of Smithville and county of Brunswick, and much interest in the subject of education was developed, which resulted in a liberal subscription by many of the permanent citizens of the county.

Dr. Frederick J. Hill, of Orton Plantation, contributed three hundred dollars, and the other rich planters on the Cape Fear contributed from fifty to two hundred dollars each. Mr. John C. Swain and Mr. McRacken, contributed liberally, and Mr. Daniel L. Russell, Sr., contributed two hundred dollars. St. Johns Lodge No. 110 of Free Masons, being about to lose their rooms in the old court house, by reason of that building being torn down for the purpose of erecting a new court house, contributed six hundred dollars, with the condition, that the property should be put under their charge for Lodge purposes and that a deed should be made to them by the town authorities for educational and charitable purposes as provided by the charter of the town.

The building was accordingly erected on Franklin Square, and school immediately began under the personal direction of Mr. Murphy and the Rev. J.H. Brent. The school prospered greatly for several years, and up to the beginning of the war, when it with all other schools was discontinued to await happier and more peaceful times.

During the war the building was treated very roughly being taken by the Confederate authorities for a store house for commissary supplies for the army. At the close of the war it was found to be in a wrecked and dilapidated condition, and the Masonic Lodge had gone out of existence.

It has before been stated in these papers that the Federal Navy under Capt. Cushing had broken open the Lodge and stolen the jewels, while they were engaged in the business of destroying such records of the county, as they could find in the court house. The building remained in this condition until the political crisis of reconstruction was finished and a reasonable amount of security for private and public property had been secured, and then the few surviving Masons secured a new charter for their lodge under the name of Pythagoras Lodge No. 219, and the work of repairing and rebuilding the dilapidated academy was begun by means of funds contributed by citizens of Southport and others until the building was made habitable for the purpose for which it was originated.

During the time which had elapsed since the close of the war up to the present time, a school of more or less importance has been kept in this building. Of these schools a few deserve a special mention as having laid a foundation for a good education, and a good character for many pupils. It is estimated that over fifty of the young men of Southport through the careful training and education of Rev. H.A. Daboc and his wife and Dr. Samuel W. Murphy, (the latter a son of Mr. Jeremiah Murphy before mentioned) have gone out into the world to pursue those professions for which the foundation was laid in the schools of these gentlemen. We may further add that among these boys there are two lawyers, three doctors, one professor of architecture in the University of North Carolina, one editor, one cashier of a Wilmington bank, one bank teller in a New York Trust Co., three graduates in pharmacy, and one in dentistry, several in the employment of the government, besides numerous others occupying responsible positions as book keepers and clerks in North Carolina and other states. Music has also received much attention, and pianos may now be found in many families whose children were instructed under the influence of this school.

The old court house which was originally at Lockwood's Folly, was removed to Smithville in 1805 and became the second old court house of Brunswick county, which was torn down to be replaced by a new and more modern structure built of brick in 1854 about the same time when the academy before described was erected.

While these improvements have been going on the citizens of Smithville and Southport had not neglected the building of churches

Figure 6. The Brunswick County Court House.
Photo copied with permission from *The State Port Pilot*.

and where there were only two in 1850 there are now seven of different denominations, all possessing bells of greater or less size, which ring every day of the week.

CHAPTER TWENTY-TWO

As the courts and the practice of law in Brunswick county, have been spoken of in these papers, as being entitled to the greatest respect, it seems proper that the names of the lawyers who practised in this court should have some mention as a token of remembrance of the times of peace which prevailed up to 1861. The Hon. Robt. Strange was an attorney practising in Brunswick county. He was eminent in his profession of law, and had also represented his district in Congress. He was spoken of by Franklin Pierce—afterwards as President of the United States—in a letter of introduction given to the writer in 1847 as "my valued friend Strange" and there seemed to be much affection between these two men. Col. Robert Strange, son of above mentioned gentleman, and his partner Duncan K. McRae practised in the courts of Brunswick, both being men of real ability, Thomas C. Miller, Dave B. Baker, Manger London, John L. Holmes and Robert L. French who was afterward Judge, and was distinguished for his ability as a lawyer, for his gentle and social qualities, and who had the courtly manners of the olden time gentleman, and was greatly beloved by his host of friends. The Hon. George Davis, afterwards the Attorney General of the Confederate States, honored and beloved by his friends and associates to the last of his life, and Moody B. Smith, a lawyer of ability, was a member of the Brunswick bar and practised here until the close of the war when he removed to the city of New York. Duncan J. Devane, Alfred M. Waddell and Col. Charles M. Stedman, also practised in Brunswick County; also the Hon. Samuel J. Person, a man of great ability in the legal profession, was elected a judge of the Superior Court of law, which position he held with honor to himself and credit to the state.

There are so many others connected with the legal profession in Brunswick County, that it is impossible to mention the names of all of them. Nearly all of those whose names are herein subscribed have passed away leaving honorable records of their distinguished service to their clients and to the country.

The period of time embraced in these reminiscences is that between 1848 to 1900 or over a half a century. The half century, which preceded this one, was a most interesting period in the history of North Carolina, many of the actors and public events of that period have been ably detailed by Col. Alfred M. Waddell, Mr. James Sprunt and others, and the history written by them continues as records of great men and great deeds which honored themselves and the nation, and has given to North Carolina a high position in every branch of law, science, medicine, poetry and fiction.

Great changes are now impending over the political condition of State and Nation, and it is impossible to foretell what the result may be; and it is safe to say that no half century of the nation's history can be more interesting or more pregnant with great events, than the one which these pages imperfectly describe.

During the time when the turpentine industry engrossed a large part of the business of eastern North Carolina, agriculture was at a low ebb; the decline of this industry has led to the substitution of a new kind of agriculture, more varied and interesting in every respect than that which existed when the pine tree occupied so much of the attention of the land owners of Eastern North Carolina. Great plantations have been divided into smaller ones and new lands have been brought into cultivation. Neat cottages have been built in large numbers and the smaller farms have been fenced with durable fences, so that in some places the whole face of the country appears like an immense market garden. Better stock has replaced the old and most of the farmers pride themselves upon their fine stock of cattle, horses and mules, which the profits of their trucking industry enables them to possess. The improvements in agriculture is so great it would take much space to detail it. When these farmers shall be able to see their way clear to dispose of the thousands of worthless cur dogs, so as to add sheep husbandry to the other labors of the farm, and the "razor back" hog shall disappear from the forest, and trees of all kinds will be permitted to spring up and grow, then we may confidently predict that eastern North Carolina will be the garden spot of the world. While these improvements are going on, and in process of development there will be time to find out that there are classes of persons whose brains cannot be developed to any great extent, and it is a waste of time and money to try to make preachers, lawyers, doctors and school masters out of men whose highest development could only make them skillful in the development of the soil, some ideas of a political nature, which go by the names of prohibition, will be smoothed away to such an extent, that the grape vine and its products will be one of the most beautiful and profitable of all the farmers crops, adding millions of dollars to the value of his property, and giving him that one of nature's products which is more often spoken of in that Great Book which should be the rule and guide of every one's faith viz: The Holy Bible.

Let us hope that the apple, the peach and every variety of fruit which grows so luxuriously in a large part of North Carolina will be added to the farmers productions; that above all, the interests of sheep husbandry shall be cultivated, and many more thousands of dollars be added to the farmers purse. These last mentioned products all are possible when agriculture is varied.

The next great changes which have come to pass during the period of which these chapters have been written is of course the period of war, in which the Cape Fear section took prominent position. The far reaching effects of the war between the States has already taken many schemes, written by able historians of the times, and will take many more schemes before the effects of that great contest can be described in detail. At the time when these reminiscences were begun, North Carolina and every part of it, was indeed a happy land, its inhabitants both male and female were filled with love for their country, and the fires of patriotism burned in every breast. The changes made by war which penetrated every home, and every fire side have not changed that lofty patriotism which existed before the war, and although for a few short years the citizens of North Carolina and the south generally gave their entire energies to the war, for principles which they believed to be just. They still believe in their country and the whole of it as the "land of the free, and the home of the brave," and they love it with abiding devotion, but they cannot forget, that they fought for a principle which seemed to them to be just and right. They will never forget the dear ones who fought so bravely, so many of whom lie buried beneath the soil, but these memories do not make them less true to the country which is again reunited by ties which can never again be broken.

—o—

Index

WALTER GILMAN CURTIS

Walter Curtis was born in the New Hampshire town of Hopkinton on May 10, 1826. His father Nathaniel Curtis had moved there in 1820, met and married Lydia H. Fowler, Walter's mother. Nathaniel, a prominent citizen of the town, represented Hopkinton in the Legislature for four terms. He was also a business partner to the Gilman store next door.

Walter attended Hopkinton Academy and enrolled at Dartmouth College in 1842. After the sophomore fall term he left college and in the spring of 1844 took a position as tutor in Mecklenburg, Virginia. This to earn the necessary tuition money. In 1845 he returned to Concord, New Hampshire and worked as a medical student in the office of Dr. Timothy Hayden. He studied under Dr. Hayden for three years, and also attended one course of medical lectures at the Massachusetts Medical College, the medical department of Harvard University.

In 1849 Walter arrived in Southport where, while hoping to complete his medical studies and to graduate, he entered a fairly large medical practice and now found it impossible to break away. He spent his medial career—and his remaining life—"in that ancient town."

Dr. Curtis was appointed acting Assistant Surgeon in the U.S. Army in 1852 and remained in that position for a year. Following the Civil War he was appointed Quarantine Medical Officer for the Cape Fear River by the military government. He held this position for the next thirty years. When civil government was re-established, Governor Holden appointed him Quarantine Physician in 1868, an office he held until the quarantine service was taken over by the U.S. Marine Hospital Service in 1895.

In the first election after restoration of civil government in the state, in 1867, Curtis was elected Clerk of the Superior Court of Brunswick County, North Carolina. In December 1866 Dr. Curtis, along with Stephen B. Thurston and Archie M. Guthrie were the first officers of the newly chartered Pythagoras Masonic Lodge No. 249 in Southport. Curtis also served as Southport's Mayor in 1875-76.

His first marriage to Sarah Copeland, daughter of the Rev. Enoch Pratt, on January 10, 1855 ended tragically when she died, four and a half years later, on January 31, 1861. They had no children.

He married Sarah Twining on January 10, 1866, again the daughter of a cleric, the Rev. Joshua Wingate Weeks. Again his wife died. This on December 25, 1875, and once more he was alone.

Margaret Johnston Coit, who had been bride's maid at his wedding to Sarah Twining, entered his life shortly afterwards. They were engaged in 1877 and married on May 9, 1878. She was the daughter of Dr. Benjamin B. Coit and Adelaide Johnson.

Figure 7. Gravestone at the Oakdale Cemetery in Wilmington, North Carolina.
Photo by Wolfgang Furstenau

Walter and Margaret had four children. A girl named Margaret died in infancy. Three boys, Clarence Walter, Nathaniel Cortlandt and Howard Coit were born on, respectively, December 17, 1879, February 8, 1881 and October 8, 1882.

His Alma Mater, Dartmouth, awarded him an AB degree in 1897. After nearly 50 years it restored for him the "honor of membership," as he put it, in the class of '46.

In 1905 the booklet *Reminiscences of Wilmington and Smithville-- Southport* was published by his son Howard, then publisher of the Southport Herald. It was soft-bound, 5½ by 8½ inches in size. The 62-page text was set in two 2⅛ inch columns. Opposite the title page was a 2 by 2¾ inch portrait of the author, Dr. Walter G. Curtis.

Curtis died at his home in Southport, North Carolina on August 9, 1909 following a severe stroke six weeks prior. Mrs. Margaret Curtis remained in Southport until she, too, died on March 7, 1923. Both are buried at the Oakdale Cemetery in Wilmington, along with their son Howard.

Wolfgang Furstenau
Editor